W9-CAO-147

THE CONCISE GUIDE TO
COPY EDITING

Preparing
Written
Work for
Readers

By
Paul
LaRocque

Library of Congress Cataloging-in-Publication Data

LaRocque, Paul, 1931-
   Concise guide to copy editing : preparing written work
for readers /
by Paul LaRocque.
      p. cm.
   ISBN 0-9729937-1-1
   1. Journalism--Editing. 2. Copy-reading. I. Title.
   PN4778.L37 2003
   808'.06607--dc21

                              2003008973

ISBN 0-9729937-1-1
Printed in U.S.A.
Printing 10 9 8 7 6 5 4 3 2 1

Marion Street Press, Inc.
PO Box 2249
Oak Park, IL 60304
708-445-8330
www.marionstreetpress.com

The relationship between writer and editor is often bloody. But no writer ever had a better friend than Paul LaRocque and his 'plainly spoken' style of editing. More importantly, no reader ever had a better friend.

STEVE BLOW, COLUMNIST, DALLAS MORNING NEWS

In **The Concise Guide to Copy Editing***, veteran journalist and teacher Paul LaRocque gives copy editors what they most desperately need: love. Don't get me wrong. This book is no Valentine. It's a set of tools, sharpened in the interests of readers. The love comes from the author's abiding respect, an attitude that holds the craft of copy editing in highest regard.*

ROY PETER CLARK, SENIOR SCHOLAR, POYNTER INSTITUTE

Paul LaRocque is a master teacher. Few editors can teach lessons with such clarity. Paul is able to take the complicated, dissect it with surgeon-like skill and make it register with even the least engaged student.

BOB RAY SANDERS, COLUMNIST, FORT WORTH STAR-TELEGRAM

As a writing coach and journalism teacher, I am greatly impressed with Paul LaRocque's approach to copy editing. He obviously cares about 'the story' and brings his reader step by step on the journey to strengthen the narrative. This is a book not only for beginning copy editors but surely for experienced ones as well.

PAUL SALSINI, MILWAUKEE JOURNAL-SENTINEL

How many times have you read a news story and grumbled, 'Didn't anyone edit this?' Paul LaRocque helps out aggravated readers by providing a systematic way for copy editors to inject clarity into fuzzy news stories. **The Concise Guide to Copy Editing** *recognizes that copy editing often requires delicate surgery, rather than mere slashing and hacking. LaRocque provides instructions about how to artfully wield the scalpel.*

PHILIP SEIB, PROFESSOR OF JOURNALISM, MARQUETTE UNIVERSITY

This book offers insightful tips reporters usually don't get, unless they're sitting beside an editor who cares enough to explain why each change in copy has been made.

LARRY L. ROSE, PUBLISHER, CORPUS CHRISTI CALLER-TIMES

For Paula, and for my brother, Ray, whom I
followed into journalism.

Contents

1: Why do we need editors?

2: Where do you start?

3: A sense of order

4: A fresh start

5: Tighter, please

Introduction

This book is about words, so let's talk briefly about the words that describe the task we are about to discuss — *copy editing*.

Copy editing is what newspapers and others in the publishing business call that last check on written work before it goes to print. *Copy* is the word publications use for what writers produce. *Editing* is the act of preparing the writers' work for publication. Copy and editing are two of the most important elements in the feeding of readers. The most important, of course, is the raw material — the idea that begins the process. This book is about more than copy editing. It's about satisfying readers — the consumers of information and ideas. Consider this book a marketing guide for editors.

Imagine for a moment that you are in the restaurant business. Smart restaurateurs know their customers will come back if they employ creative chefs who provide top quality food. Editors are like restaurant managers — they want to please customers and keep the chef happy. If you want your business to succeed, you've got to demand quality produce (ideas) from your suppliers, employ creative chefs (writers), and know your customers (readers). You must think like customers and anticipate their needs and tastes.

Restaurateurs are first tasters, making certain diners are served quality food. Editors are first readers, making sure readers get quality writing. As first readers, editors are also *proxy* readers. They have reader consent to demand quality writing, prepare it tastefully, and serve it appealingly. If editors do their job well, both readers and writers are pleased. That's not an easy task. Editors are the mediators between writer and reader, insisting on clear and concise communication. Editing is a cooperative effort, and its importance increases daily as the world moves with light speed into the Information Age. What is said in Peoria can be read in Pakistan in seconds.

Good editing isn't achieved by formula alone. Like food preparation, a recipe helps, but ingredients and skill make a story appealing. Of course, stories must be grammatically correct, accurate, and adhere to style. They also must be organized, easy to read, and interesting. And pertinent detail is important, but detail alone will not attract and retain readers. Above all, stories should be appealing. Once you've found what readers want, serve it. But be flexible — tastes change.

When I first began editing at newspapers, I concentrated on mechanics, obvious holes in a story, accuracy, legal aspects, style, etc. — the things editing textbooks stress. They are important. However, in time, I realized that readers expect more than just "clean" writing. I also realized that I was not the final judge of an article's quality — the reader is. I began to look more closely at organization, transition, sentence and paragraph structure, precision, and voice. I had become a proxy reader. Of course, most readers don't consciously consider all those factors. If a story is organized, clear, and concise, they will probably read and enjoy without giving much thought to why.

I realized that I was a first reader after several years of being a formula editor. Like most editors, I honed my skills in college classrooms with the help of textbooks and fussy professors and later in a newsroom under scrutiny of demanding desk editors. I considered myself a good editor. But I was a formula editor. I was not a first reader.

I don't know exactly when I began sitting in the reader's chair. It didn't happen overnight. Years of listening to reader phone calls about stories they misunderstood, being cornered by hostile readers at parties, and questioned about stories by friends and neighbors may have helped push me into that chair. Once seated, I began to read my newspaper differently. I was not willing to suffer through wordy leads, to reread fuzzy passages, to attempt to interpret rambling quotations, and to return to the top of a story when I became lost in tangled sentences. I wanted information. I wanted my questions answered. Style and mechanics were no longer the major considerations. I recall a tongue-in-cheek anecdote from a former newspaper editing colleague. It went something like this: "On the bus this morning, everyone was talking about whether adviser was spelled with an *er* or *or.*"

Imagine that the story you are editing is a conversation on a bus. *Talk* to readers. A good story is a conversation with readers. If your story is not "plainly spoken," all its good information may be lost. Only the most dedicated readers will try to untangle it. The rest will ignore it. Listening to readers and writers has helped me become a better editor, and it will help you, too. Like that good restaurateur, you will come to know both your customers and your chefs.

Seek criticism. It's vital if you truly want to improve. I'm extremely fortunate to have a live-in critic — my wife, Paula. She has encouraged, inspired, and edited my work. I owe her special thanks, too, for providing much of the grammar comment in Chapter 7. I've also been fortunate to have journalism colleagues who have been harsh, honest, and helpful. And writers, both student and professional, have taught me much. One in particular I remember well. Charlie House was an imaginative feature writer for *The Milwaukee Journal.* I removed a word from one of his stories, and the next day he wanted to know why.

"Because it's not a word," I told him. "I looked it up, and it's not in the dictionary." He replied, "It is a word. It's *my* word."

It was a short lesson on the proxy reader's need to be open and flexible.

This book, a guide for all editors who want to please readers, offers a short cut to becoming a proxy reader. It touches on such necessary fundamentals as grammar, spelling, etc., but concentrates on structure and clarity — *editing for readers.* With few exceptions, the stories and passages appearing here were published in various media; I've changed names and places in some cases. At the end of each chapter are exercises that can be done on your own, in newsroom seminars or discussion groups, or in journalism classrooms. The book is not so much a how-to book as it is a do-it-yourself book. As such, it's a work of tried-and-true principles, ideas, and suggestions. I hope you'll consider them, adapt some, adopt some, and become a good first reader.

Paul R. LaRocque
August 2003
Arlington, Texas

Chapter 1

Why do we need editors?
To help readers, of course

If language is not correct,
then what is said is not what is meant;
if what is said is not meant,
then what ought to be done remains undone;
if this remains undone,
then morals and art deteriorate;
if morals and art deteriorate,
justice will go astray;
if justice goes astray,
the people will stand about in helpless confusion.
Hence there must be no arbitrariness in what is said.
This matters above everything.
— Confucius

Readers do not like surprises. That is perhaps the most important thing an editor should know. An article that advertises itself as a report on federal defense spending must deal with just that and answer as quickly and clearly as possible any questions the story's headline and lead raise. The story information should unfold logically and smoothly, like a conversation. First, of course, the writer must anticipate and answer reader questions; then, editors must ensure that all reader questions — within reason — are answered clearly and precisely. Editors, the proxy readers, are the quality control personnel of the publishing business. Every story — like any consumer product — should pass the quality test before it's released to readers.

It's not too much to ask that a story be as close to perfect as possible. Publishing standards should be no less than those for any business. We expect restaurateurs to serve expertly prepared food, accountants to complete our tax returns without error, automakers to produce cars that run perfectly, and lawyers to present our cases flawlessly. They, too, work under deadline pressures. So why should we expect less than perfection from newspapers, magazines, online publications, and other mass media? Misinformation can be as harmful or costly as a bad meal, an incorrect tax return, a defective car, or a lost lawsuit. It is especially important today that mass media make a greater effort to be clear and accurate because today's world moves on information. This is the Information Age when billions, no matter how remote their location, have access to news, data, and entertainment with the flick of a switch or touch of a keyboard. The speed and breadth of communication make clarity even more important. A faulty financial story can damage a company and cost employees jobs and investors money.

Stories that fail the reader test should not be published. Editors should, with writer help, repair defective stories or postpone their publication. Paraphrase the old slogan from a wine company: "I will publish no story before its time." In making repairs, an editor must be absolutely certain that the writer's intent is not ignored or circumvented, that the writer's voice is not lost, and that readers are satisfied. That's not easy. And it seldom can be done alone. Writer collaboration, while not always possible, is still critical.

On some newspaper editing desks, for example, an editor may handle stories produced by staff writers along with stories that come from around the world. The latter are commonly called wire news, and they may come from The Associated Press or several other services that provide news and feature coverage in areas outside the paper's circulation area — state, regional, national and international coverage. Editor dealings with staff writers can be relatively simple. Most of the time, staff writers are in the office or within easy reach by phone or e-mail. Wire service writers are generally not easy to reach. They are scattered around the world. But wire service editors are usually just a quick phone call or e-mail message away. We'll discuss more specifically editing wire stories in a later chapter.

Whatever the origin of the article, editing standards should be the same: The story must be clear and easy to read. If it is not, it should not be published. What does it say for a medium's quality and integrity if it offers readers a shoddy product? It certainly does not build trust or readership.

To ensure a quality product, editors sometimes may have to make changes in a story without consulting the author. Such editing should be done with utmost care. If there is the slightest doubt about the author's intent, the story should be held until the author can explain the vague passage, or the vague passage should be cut, if possible, without harming the story. Blind editing, or no editing at all, of vague passages does nothing for the reader and may damage the writer's and the medium's credibility. Thus, editor-writer cooperation is essential and should not be circumvented except in extreme circumstances. Time is essential in highly competitive news situations, but time should not trump accuracy and clarity.

Ideally, editors and writers should be partners and

friends. Often, the opposite seems to be true. Editors gripe and say writers are careless; writers complain that editors ruin their stories. In truth, they need each other — for the readers' sake. If it were possible, every writer should have a personal editor. And published articles should have not only a writer's byline but an editor's credit line. That not being practical for many publications, editors should try to know as much as possible about each staff writer they work with. While editors must have high standards, they should be flexible enough to permit writers to experiment — within reason. Formula writing produces dull reading, and innovation and fresh writing cannot thrive in rigid environments. Editors should help writers break through convention to produce sparkling, fresh prose. Generally, they should recommend changes in writers' stories instead of making them. And when an editor does make changes, the changes should be explained — either at the time they are made or after the story has been published.

Editors and writers should talk often. They might eat lunch together occasionally. Or organize discussion groups and talk about writing and editing, not just writing in their publication but in other newspapers, magazines, and books — non-fiction and fiction. Both should keep journals. They should clip articles they like and dislike and discuss why, first in their journals and later with each other.

Anyone who makes a living in the writing professions should be an avid reader. Reading will help you become a better editor. When you see good writing, ask yourself why you like it. When you read poor writing, ask why it's poor. Share your thoughts with the writers you edit. Send them notes, talk about writing at lunch and at coffee breaks. And be liberal with compliments. You don't have to be a dullard who thinks and talks only of work, but you do need to practice what you do. Professional athletes, musicians, and actors do not improve by merely performing before an audience. They study the work of others, make notes on methods they can borrow, critique their own work, talk with others in their profession, and they experiment. Editors and writers also perform for an audience — readers. They owe it to readers to be as professional as athletes, musicians, and actors. Audiences have a choice. If the performance is substandard, they will not participate. Without readers, writers and editors are tossing words into the wind.

Editors need not be good writers themselves — although that helps — but they must be able to recognize good writing and to suggest ways to make good writing better. They also should be able to recognize bad writing and to tactfully reject it or suggest ways to improve it. Good writers need little help and are usually receptive to an editor's suggestions. Mediocre and poor writers are often the most difficult to work with. They sometimes are insecure and defensive and need encouragement and patience if they are to improve. Editors may have to accept some mediocre writing, particularly with insecure writers, in order to encourage improvement — but such acceptance cannot be at reader expense. Writing can be mediocre, but still clear and precise. Such writing should never be accepted without tactful comment, however. Make suggestions for improvement after deadline and perhaps at lunch. Bad writing is another matter and should never be accepted.

Editor criticism should be measured and careful. Constant put-down often results in continued mediocre writing or worse. Editors can best help problem writers by asking questions, making suggestions, and encouraging writers to develop a stronger writing voice. Regular contact, such as in informal writer-editor discussion groups, helps soften criticism and provides a friendly forum.

Wow, you say. That's a lot to ask of an editor. It's not a lot if you want to keep and gain readers. The editor who thinks only of meeting deadlines is a manager, not an editor. Deadlines are important, but the tail shouldn't wag the dog. Quality is first. Actors who forget lines or whose performance lacks credibility, soon find that no one is watching them. Similarly, readers will not read publications they neither trust nor enjoy. Meet deadlines, but don't push through bad writing in order to meet them. Good stories are just as good the next day.

Those suggestions may seem radical to some, especially to formula editors. Applying them will not be easy. Good writing requires hard work by both writer and editor. As Hemingway said, "Easy writing makes damn hard reading." This book is for all editors and would-be editors and perhaps writers who are willing to work hard at making their media more readable, exciting, and interesting. It is not a complete course in editing. It is merely a guide for improvement. It suggests ways to recognize weak writing and ways to improve it. It should make the editor think about writing and react as a reader.

You may ask, "Who has time for all this?" The answer: Make time. Don't try to do everything at once. Take it step by step. Form good editing habits. Give the most critical problems priority, and squeeze the others in when you can. Change won't come overnight, and some may resist your efforts and ideas, but change and improvement will come if you are patient and sincere. It has to come. Without readers, you have no job.

"Ideas often lie unused because people do not want to use them. The fact that something is possible does not mean it will happen." (The words of economist Lester C. Thurow as quoted by Thomas L. Friedman in *The Lexus and the Olive Tree*.)

In the following chapters, we'll discuss some suggestions for making writing clear and concise.

Exercises

• Organize a group of writers and editors. If you are a working journalist, invite some writers to provide stories to critique. Pair writers with editors. If you are a journalism instructor, set up pairings with a writing class or the student newspaper writers. Don't worry if you have more writers than editors or editors than writers. Double up. An editor can handle two writers or a writer can work with two editors.

The exercise objective is to create constructive dialogue between editor and writer.

Writers should submit one of their best stories. Editors should have time — overnight or a couple of days — to critique the stories.

This exercise won't work if editors and writers are not frank and sincere. Not everything editors suggest will be practical, and some writer reactions will be defensive. When those situations arise, speak up. Discuss it. Compromise — but keep readers in mind.

After the critique session, writers will rewrite their stories. Keep both the original revised versions. Meet again and repeat the earlier critique process. Discuss the changes, improvements, and shortcomings.

• The next step: Recruit "readers" from a non-news department in your company or from a non-journalism department in school. Give the two versions of the story to the readers and ask them to write a brief comparison critique, indicating which version was easiest to read and informative.

Meet again — with the reader present, if possible — and discuss the reader critique. If readers indicate a need for improvement, discuss ways to implement improvements. Remember, readers are the consumers of your words, and they won't buy a product they don't like.

Chapter 2

Where do you start?
At the beginning

*Begin at the beginning . . . and go on till you come to
the end: then stop.*
—Lewis Carroll

Don't begin editing a story before you have read it to
the end. That may seem like an unnecessary caution, but
sometimes rushed editors may edit while reading the story
for the first time. When you edit on first reading, you may
be wasting time by making changes that will not be necessary if you reorganize the story, or you may make errors
because you don't know the whole story. Know the story
and its focus before you begin editing. The time spent on
a first reading is not wasted, and it may even save time.
The first reading helps you to make quick decisions to
change or move passages during your second reading.
Deadlines should be met, but not by allowing substandard
stories to be published. Readers will not know you were
rushed; they will know only that the story is poor. They
won't care why it is poor; they will care only that it is poor.
And they won't want it. So don't give it to them.

First read the story for content, flow, and focus. If you

choose, mark spots that need work as you go. You can do this easily on your screen by using a different type style or color — something easy to recognize when you go back to check details. Finding errors, fixing mechanics, or improving passages is not your goal on the first reading. You should act like a reader. The first reading should tell you how much work may be needed to make the story reader friendly. Look for bumps in your reading road.

Ask yourself questions — the things that readers want to know as they move through the story. What's the story about? Why should I care? What do I want to know? Don't stop to repair imperfect passages — you'll lose your focus. Remember, the story is a conversation between the writer and you. If you have questions, write them on your screen at the top of the story, or in a different type style or color in the story. If the story seems disorganized, jot down suggestions as you read. And if the story is confusing, you can mark wayward passages. Those markings may help if you have to reorganize the story. You can also develop a shorthand for marking to save you time. For example, you can use *tr* for lack of transition, *gr* for grammar error, *sp* for spelling, *gtp* for get to the point, *?* for a passage that doesn't track or make sense, etc.

When you've read the story through, it's time to decide whether you can repair the story or not. If the repairs are minor, move to the next step in the editing process. If the story requires major changes, note them and consult the author. Or if the story came to your desk by way of a department editor, consult the department editor. Some newspapers encourage direct discussion between copy editor and writer. It's easy today, because it can be done online. Others require that a department editor handle copy editor questions. Whatever the system, major changes in a story should not be made without consulting the author. If that's not possible, ask that the story be held. Faulty stories do not please readers, and they damage the credibility of the publication.

Enough preaching. Let's practice. Here are two short wire stories. They are light, published more for entertainment than news. So they should be concise, which they are. They also should be well-organized and move quickly, not wasting words. What can you do to make them better reading? Read them first, and then make changes if they are needed. Remember, you're acting as a reader in the first round. Forget about being an editor for a while. You're a reader. Here's the first story as it came to your desk.

For practice, you may want to mark this story during your first reading. Then you can compare your notes to the marked version that follows the original story.

Lips
(121 words)

WASHINGTON — The gesture is unlikely to make a dent in the federal deficit, but the maker of a new board game called "Read My Lips" thought it might be able to sell a few more games if it offered to contribute.

Pressman Toy Corp. of New York has pledged to donate $1 from the sale of each $17 game to the federal government to help reduce the nation's $152 billion deficit.

The board game, whose title was the campaign rallying cry for President Bush in his pledge not to raise taxes, involves one partner trying to guess the words being mouthed by another.

The promotion is good from June 25 through July 4, to give the gimmick an Independence Day angle.

Now, let's put on our reader hats. Here are my comments on the story as I do the first reading. The comments are lengthy for sake of clarity. In your first reading, you probably won't have as much to say about the story, and you'll probably use shorthand markings.

Story:

WASHINGTON — The gesture is unlikely to make a dent in the federal deficit, but the maker of a new board game called "Read My Lips" thought it might be able to sell a few more games if it offered to contribute.

Reader:

What gesture? Tell me about the gesture before you tell me what it will or will not do. Get to the point. "Contribute" to what?

Story:

Pressman Toy Corp. of New York has pledged to donate $1 from the sale of each $17 game to the federal government to help reduce the nation's $152 billion deficit.

Reader:

Oh, that's it. The company will give part of its profit to help cut the deficit. But why is it doing that? What's the game's connection to the federal deficit?

Story:

The board game, whose title was the campaign rallying cry for President Bush in his pledge not to raise taxes, involves one partner trying to guess the words being mouthed by another.

Reader:

Yes, I see the connection now. Why didn't you say that?

Story:

The promotion is good from June 25 through July 4, to give the gimmick an Independence Day angle.

Reader:

Why Independence Day? Is it independence from debt or merely a patriotic gesture?

Change hats. Now you're the editor, and you're ready for the second round. As a reader you moved quickly through the story and had some questions, which you made note of or indicated by marking the copy. First, what is the focus? Is it a new board game? Is it a promotion gimmick? Is it the federal deficit? The focus includes all those factors — it's the gesture. Perhaps you need to move up the gesture background information from the second paragraph — the $1 donation to help pay the federal deficit. Then, what can you do about the Independence Day gimmick? Is the rest of the story organized? Do the developments follow logically from the focus sentence — the lead? Let's take another look at the story and do some editing. (New wording in the story is in italic type, and comments are in parentheses in bold type.)

WASHINGTON — The ~~gesture is unlikely to make a dent in the federal deficit, but the~~ maker of a new board game called "Read My Lips" ~~thought it might be able to sell a few more games if it offered to contribute.~~ (**Get to the point. Readers want to know the gesture. Avoid the obvious — that it won't make a dent in the deficit and that it's a promotion. And it's opinion.**)
~~Pressman Toy Corp. of New York~~ has pledged ~~to donate~~ $1 from the sale of each ~~$17~~ game ~~to the federal government~~ to help reduce the nation's $152 billion deficit. (**Explain the gesture. Give the company name later. You don't need both *pledge* and *donate*. Get rid**

**of one. Move the game's price to a more conven-
ient spot.)**

Pressman Toy Corp. of New York makes the board game,
whose title was the campaign ~~rallying cry~~ *slogan* for
President Bush in his pledge not to raise taxes. *The game
sells for $17 and* involves one partner trying to guess ~~the~~
words ~~being~~ mouthed by another. **(Now you can use the
name. Change** *rallying cry* **to** *slogan.* **It's shorter and
not a cliché. Create two sentences and get the price
in the second. Save a word, too. You don't need** *the*
or *being.***)**

The promotion is good from June 25 through *the
Fourth of July* ~~July 4,~~ to give the gimmick *a patriotic* ~~an
Independence Day~~ angle. **(Make it** *Fourth of July* **so you
have the date and day in a capsule. Instead of the**
Independence Day **angle, make it a** *patriotic* **angle —
it's shorter and states the angle clearly. Strike the
comma before** *to give.***)**

Let's look at the edited product. It's complete but much
shorter — 91 words compared to 121 in the original.

WASHINGTON —The maker of a new board
game called "Read My Lips" has pledged $1 from
the sale of each game to help reduce the nation's
$152 billion deficit.

Pressman Toy Corp. of New York makes the
board game, whose title was the campaign slogan
for President Bush in his pledge not to raise taxes.
The game sells for $17 and involves one partner
trying to guess words mouthed by another.

The promotion is good from June 25 through the
Fourth of July to give the gimmick a patriotic angle.

For a short piece, that story required quite a bit of
work. Editing isn't always tearing up the foundation and

building anew. Sometimes a story needs only a few subtle changes to make it smoother and easy to read. Here's another short story, also about a board game and money, but the setting is entirely different. It has a bit of conflict — the crime angle — along with the bizarre or entertainment factor. Let's read it first as a reader. Again, you may want to mark this original version and compare your notes to mine in the marked version that follows.

ATM
(139 words)

ATLANTIC CITY, N.J. – Remember the Monopoly game card that read, "Bank error in your favor, collect $200"?

It really happened in Atlantic City, in the city that inspired the board game. An automated teller machine in a casino began spitting out $100 bills instead of $20s.

But authorities warned that those who keep the money might need a "Get out of jail free" card.

Customers lined up as the PNC Bank machine at The Grand mistakenly flipped out about $85,000 over a few hours Thursday night and Friday morning. Casino workers were among those cashing in.

Hotel security finally shut down the machine. How many people withdrew money and how the mistake occurred weren't known. But the ATM will be able to provide a list of the people who got cash. And they will have to return the money.

Now, let's mark the story as we scan it as a reader.

Story:
ATLANTIC CITY, N.J. – Remember the Monopoly

game card that read, "Bank error in your favor, collect $200"?

Reader:

Yes, I remember. What about it?

Story:

It really happened in Atlantic City, in the city that inspired the board game. An automated teller machine in a casino began spitting out $100 bills instead of $20s.

Reader:

Yes, I seem to recall that the game has some connection to Atlantic City. Tell me more about that bank error.

Story:

But authorities warned that those who keep the money might need a "Get out of jail free" card.

Reader:

Why is that? But tell me about that bank error. What happened? Who got the money?

Story:

Customers lined up as the PNC Bank machine at The Grand mistakenly flipped out about $85,000 over a few hours Thursday night and Friday morning. Casino workers were among those cashing in.

Reader:

Wow! So what's going to happen now?

Story:

Hotel security finally shut down the machine. How many people withdrew money and how the mistake occurred weren't known. But the ATM will be able to provide a list of the people who got cash. And they will have to return the money.

Reader:

So now they'll have to give it back or face prosecution? Perhaps they'll need that "Get out of jail free" card.

Change into your editor's hat again. As a reader you moved quickly through the story and had your questions answered. When you came to the end, your thoughts went back to the third paragraph, the one about authorities and the jail card. Perhaps that sentence will fit better at the end. It answers the question raised in the last paragraph. As the third paragraph, it interrupts the conversation about what happened. Let's move it and see how it looks.

ATLANTIC CITY, N.J. – Remember the Monopoly game card that read, "Bank error in your favor, collect $200"?

It really happened in Atlantic City, in the city that inspired the board game. An automated teller machine in a casino began spitting out $100 bills instead of $20s.

Customers lined up as the PNC Bank machine at The Grand mistakenly flipped out about $85,000 over a few hours Thursday night and Friday morning. Casino workers were among those cashing in.

Hotel security finally shut down the machine. How many people withdrew money and how the mistake occurred weren't known. But the ATM will be able to provide a list of the people who got cash. And they will have to return the money.

But authorities warned that those who keep the money might need a "Get out of jail free" card.

That's better. Now let's go back and see if we can tighten it, make it stronger, or make it flow more smoothly. Here it is again with comments on the editing in bold type.

ATLANTIC CITY, N.J. – Remember the Monopoly game card that read, "Bank error in your favor, collect $200"?

It really happened in Atlantic City, ~~in~~ the city that inspired the board game. An automated teller machine in a casino began ~~spitting out~~ *giving customers* $100 bills instead of $20s. (**Cut** *in*; **it's deadwood. Cut** *spitting out* **and insert** *giving customers.* **That little change gets people in the picture. The machine didn't just start spitting out money. Customers had to initiate the transactions. And you don't need a paragraph here. The topic hasn't changed. Run the two paragraphs together.**) Customers lined up as the PNC Bank machine at The Grand ~~mistakenly~~ flipped out about $85,000 over a few hours Thursday night and Friday morning. Casino workers were among those cashing in. (*Mistakenly* **is redundant.**)

Hotel security finally shut down the machine. How many people withdrew money and how the mistake occurred weren't known. But the ATM will be able to provide a list of the people who got cash. And, authorities warned, ~~they will have to return the money. But authorities warned that~~ those who keep the money might need a "Get out of jail free" card. (**A little pruning and combining makes the last paragraph tighter. You don't have to say customers must return the money if you say they might need the jail card if they keep it.**)

Now, here's how it looks: Tighter — 129 words compared to 139 in the original — and a bit easier to read.

ATLANTIC CITY, N.J. – Remember the Monopoly game card that read, "Bank error in your favor, collect $200"?

It really happened in Atlantic City, the city that inspired the board game. An automated teller machine in a casino began giving customers $100 bills instead of $20s. Customers lined up as the PNC Bank machine at The Grand flipped out about $85,000 over a few hours Thursday night and Friday morning. Casino workers were among those cashing in.

Hotel security finally shut down the machine. How many people withdrew money and how the mistake occurred weren't known. But the ATM will be able to provide a list of the people who got cash. And, authorities warned, those who keep the money might need a "Get out of jail free" card.

You've just made a good, entertaining story better with very little work. You helped readers get the answers to their questions quickly and in a logical and easy-to-read order. Chapter 3 presents a story that requires more work before it can be stamped *reader acceptable*.

Exercises

• Find a published story of no more than six paragraphs and edit it. Focus on tightening and improving readability. Insert "reader" comments, using the examples in this chapter as models.

• Read again the ATM story above. No story has just one way to tell it. Rewrite the story to about the same length, using a different lead and approach. Compare your rewritten story to the original. Explain your revision and why you chose your format. Now try the same process with the Lips story.

Chapter 3

A sense of order:
Logical development pleases
readers

A whole is that which has beginning, middle, and end.
— Aristotle

You begin most conversations with something to pique your listener's interest. And then you usually bring up the developments in a logical order. If you don't, then your listener will interrupt you and say, "Wait a minute. You just said . . . ." Then you'll have to go back and fill in the missing detail or bring into the conversation something you had planned to save for later. Or you may say, "Be patient; I'm coming to that." If you want listeners to be patient, you have to prepare them with foreshadowing and enticement, keeping their interest as you tell your story. And that requires a little thought before you talk — organizing information that builds to a climax. You may even begin the conversation with "You'll never guess what happened at the office today" — a bit of foreshadowing. Then you develop your story chronologically or logically, keeping your listener's attention, answering questions, and building to the climax: what happened at the office today. Sometimes in haste and excitement, you may rush into a conversation with bits of information in no particular order. Such excited talk is apt to be greeted by a listener's puzzled look. Disorder in print, however, will draw more than a puzzled look. The story won't be read. An editor's most important charge is to listen to the conversation and keep disorganized stories from reaching readers. Readers are not as forgiving as listeners. They cannot ask writers to start over or repeat, so they will be frustrated and probably will stop reading.

Conversation and stories develop similarly. The first conversation example in the preceding paragraph uses the pattern most news stories follow. The second, building to a climax, is usually a pattern for feature stories. However, there are all sorts of hybrids that combine elements of those two patterns. They may differ slightly in detail, but the plan is the same: orderly development of information in a manner that is easy to read.

Editors should encourage writers to organize their material before writing — to outline. They also should know how to outline so they can repair or suggest changes in disorganized stories. Making an outline is not difficult. Keep it simple. There is no need for Roman numerals, capital and small letters, etc.

Jon Franklin, Pulitzer Prize journalist and author, provides a simple outline for orderly development of long feature stories in his book *Writing for Story*. He breaks stories into three elements: complication, developments, and resolution. His outlines are short, and they use active-voice headings for each segment. Following his outline pattern, a feature story about a reunion of three sisters who were placed in foster homes when their parents were killed in an accident might look like this:

Complication:
Death separates sisters

Developments:
Families adopt girls
War disperses families
Girls marry, raise children
Story brings contact

Resolution:
Trip reunites sisters

If you change that outline a bit, you can adapt it to most stories. Instead of complication, substitute focus. Keep developments — all stories have them. Change resolution to ending — all stories must end. In some features, that ending may be a resolution, but it's still an ending. Your new outline:

Focus:
Death separates sisters

Developments:
Families adopt girls
War disperses families
Girls marry, raise children
Story brings contact

Ending:
Trip reunites sisters

You changed the labels but not the topics. Think of the outline as a map. You would not think of going into a strange city without a map or some specific directions.

Readers are word travelers. They don't want to wander, and a carefully planned story avoids wandering. The writer has primary responsibility for organizing, and the editor must attend to any disarray in a story before it reaches readers.

Even the simplest stories need organizing. Stories are easier to read when they follow a logical pattern. Some stories fit easily into patterns — routine articles such as general obituaries, meeting reports, and roundup stories such as reports on holiday traffic deaths. Traffic-death roundup stories, for example, have structural elements that don't change except for details. Reports about meetings, legislation, surveys, fires, storms, and many other multiple-element stories, are built by answering routine questions readers ask. Questions about a city council meeting might include "How am I affected?" "Why did they do that?" "When is it effective?" "What will it cost?" "Where will it be?" "Who's responsible?" "What was the vote?" If you ponder those questions before you edit, you can easily imagine an outline.

Okay, you may ask, doesn't that lead to formula writing? If editors insist that certain stories adhere to formulas, aren't they encouraging mediocrity? Isn't that what writers and editors should be trying to avoid? Yes, it is. But formula story structure is not formula writing. Formula writing depends on jargon and clichés and is stale and unnatural. Formula structure enhances fresh and innovative writing because it has built-in transitions and makes it easier for writers to concentrate on voice, vocabulary, and style.

Jon Franklin, for example, uses a formula to develop long feature stories, but his writing is fresh, and it won him a Pulitzer. So, don't confuse formula writing with formula structure. Good story structure makes it much easier to write freshly, clearly, and smoothly.

Structure is chiefly a responsibility of the author, but it's also a major concern for editors. If story structure is poor, readers suffer and are turned away. Editors, as proxy readers, must insist on easy-to-read organized stories.

Some disorganization is easily repaired. You made a few minor changes in two short wire stories in the last chapter. There was no need for discussion with the authors. Longer disorganized stories generally need major changes, and probably should be sent back to the author with suggestions for revision. Those suggestions should perhaps include a sample outline. Let's look at some simple formulas before you tackle a story that needs major reorganization.

Here's a traffic death roundup story about accidents that killed four people. Remember, this is not the only way this story can be written. The lead, for example, can mention some unusual aspects of one or more of the accidents, foreshadowing the detail that is to come later in the story. The lead may be written in two sentences or more or in two or more paragraphs. Formula structure should not inhibit flexibility, innovation, and fresh writing. It's merely a design for order. Here's the story, in outline form:

Three accidents killed four people on Wisconsin roads over the holiday weekend, including the owner of the largest dairy farm in Ashland County. The latest deaths bring the state traffic fatality total to 35 this year.

The victims:

Horace Stacatta, 58, of Ashland.

Warren Peece, 29, of Sparta.

Natalie Dressed, 30, of Sparta

Tanya Hyde, 44, of Madison.

(Details of Stacatta accident)

(Details of Peece-Dressed accident)

(Details of Hyde accident)

That formula is simple, easy to write, and it's easy for readers to follow. It is a design that can be used for any routine story that has multiple segments, such as meeting, report, and roundup stories (storm damage, etc.). Here's how such a general outline would look:

Summary lead

Summary paragraph or a sentence listing the elements A, B, and C

Details of A

Details of B

Details of C

Did you notice the similarities in the routine news outline and the feature outline? Summary lead = Focus; Details = Developments. All stories have a beginning, middle and ending. The nature of the stories makes them different. Good writers and editors will recognize the nature of stories and apply the appropriate organization.

Those routine-news outlines are easy, and an editor can usually rearrange material with minimal difficulty. However, when the story is lengthy, has a detailed or complex plot, and is disorganized, editors may need a slightly more complex outline — one similar to Franklin's model.

After you have read a disorganized story, make an outline that structures the story as readers would like to see it. Remember that in the first editing step you are a reader, and you want your questions answered as soon as they pop into your mind, or you want an explanation of why they are not answered, and when they will be. Your outline should consider the obvious reader questions, generally who, what, when, where, why, and how.

Stories that are severely disorganized, as is this next story, should go back to the author with suggestions for revision. Your suggestions should perhaps include an outline. Here's the story in its original form. It's not breaking news; it's a human-interest story about a survivor. Mark the original version if you like and compare your comments to mine, which are in the second version.

Survivor
(774 words)

By the 10th day Eleanor Clements was ready to give up.

The 69-year-old woman was stranded in a desiccated and remote corner of a cattle ranch just southwest of her home in Coal City, a community of 2,500 about 80 miles northwest of Centerville. Her husband had died four days before. And she had abandoned writing in the log that had kept her busy and hopeful, she said.

Then the search helicopter came.

Annoyed by the bugs swarming around her, and delirious, Clements thought the helicopter "looked like a big black bug in the air, a beautiful bug."

"The Lord has been so good to me," she said, weak but in good spirits as she recuperated at home from dehydration and malnourishment yesterday. "When I stop and look back, I feel very grateful. It was just a horrible ordeal."

Sunburned and bug-bitten, Clements was rescued Thursday, 10 days after she and her husband got lost on the edge of a 6,000-acre cattle ranch near the Apache River. Her 88-year-old husband, the Rev. Thomas O. Clements, died July 14. He suffered from heart disease and used a wheelchair because his diabetes prevented his knees from healing completely after several knee surgeries, she said.

The Dunbar County Medical Examiner's Office had not released the official cause of death as of yesterday, said Allison Smithson, Clements' daughter-in-law.

Married for seven years, the Coal City couple were returning July 8 from visiting friends and family in Brampton, when Eleanor Clements made a wrong turn onto the Tumbleweed Ranch. A rare rain the night before in the drought-stricken part of the state muddied the dirt road and their van got stuck. Their citizens band radio antenna had been broken by low-hanging branches, Clements said.

Hearing faint sounds of distant traffic, she honked the horn and flashed her lights until the battery died.

With no food, the couple drank two cans of Ensure, a liquid dietary supplement, diet soda that had turned flat in the heat and what water Clements could find, she said.

She stayed with her husband rather than search for help because without her help, he'd drop the cup. "Water is too valuable to waste it," she said.

"He lasted six days and that's a blessing because he was a sick man," Clements said of her husband, who was founder of House of God Church in Brampton. In 1987, he retired as pastor of Wayside Community Church in Coal City, where he will be buried tomorrow.

News reports told of wild hogs in the area, but Clements said her closest animal encounter was with a black bull.

"He stared at us and we stared at him, and he walked away," she said.

When the Rev. Clements died on the morning of July 14, she covered his body with a blanket and scattered branches on it to protect it from animals. Then she began to regroup. "I'm not just going to sit in this van and die," she said to herself.

She began to search for water and help. The only water she found was the dirty and salty rainwater she found in a creek, she said.

While looking for stray cattle, ranch intern

Bobby Ray Clampson came across the retired minister's abandoned wheelchair at the northeast end of the Tumbleweed Ranch. Later he found the diary, the van and the dead man's body.

"If the ranch hands hadn't come around, her life could have been gone too," Smithson said.

In addition to her faith, her routines of walking and water aerobics "paid off," Clements said

"If I hadn't ... I don't think I would have had the stamina" to survive, she said.

The diary that she said helped sustain her through the ordeal is still in the custody of the Grump County Sheriff's Department, said Sally Hartson, a jailer.

The couple's friends in Coal City were not alarmed by unanswered phone calls because the Clements were "always on the go," Smithson said.

"Assuming someone arrives at their home like they always do is the wrong thing to do. But you don't know that until later," Smithson said.

Smithson, 30, and her husband Rawley, 32, both of Grand Mesa, had met the Clementses in Coal City to visit, Allison Smithson said. Eleanor Clements has three sons. The Rev. Clements had two sons and four daughters, Smithson said.

Clements recently quit her job at the Coal City Tribune as a circulation employee to spend more time caring for her husband, she said.

"My son said he didn't want to leave me here alone" without a way of getting help in an emergency. I said, 'Don't worry. I'm not going anywhere.' "

Put your reader hat on again. We'll comment as we read.

Story:

By the 10th day Eleanor Clements was ready to give up.

Reader:

Who is Eleanor Clements? What's significant about the 10th day? What is she giving up and why? I realize that the answers to those questions may be coming, but I want some hint now as to what is happening. I'm annoyed that you haven't given me a clue about why I should care about Eleanor Clements' giving up. I'll read a bit more. Perhaps those questions will be answered.

Story:

The 69-year-old woman was stranded in a desiccated and remote corner of a cattle ranch just southwest of her home in Coal City, a community of 2,500 about 80 miles northwest of Centerville. Her husband had died four days before. And she had abandoned writing in the log that had kept her busy and hopeful, she said.

Reader:

OK, now I know Eleanor Clements. But why is she stranded? How did she get there? What connection does her husband's death and the log have to her situation? I'd rather have some information about how Clements got in this situation than the population of Coal City and its location. I want a reason to continue reading. She's apparently telling you this story because you attribute the last sentence to her. Where are we? Are we in her home, a police station, the ranch house, in the wild? And *desiccated* instead of *dry*? Isn't that the kind of "elegant variation" that turns a banana into an elongated yellow fruit?

Story:

Then the search helicopter came.

Reader:

OK. She's about to be rescued. But what happened to create this situation? The story seems about to end, but I have no clue as to how it started and why Eleanor has to be rescued by helicopter.

Story:
Annoyed by the bugs swarming around her, and delirious, Clements thought the helicopter "looked like a big black bug in the air, a beautiful bug."

Reader:
She's saved, and she was in pretty poor condition. But what happened to her? How did she get there?

Story:
"The Lord has been so good to me," she said, weak but in good spirits as she recuperated at home from dehydration and malnourishment yesterday. "When I stop and look back, I feel very grateful. It was just a horrible ordeal."

Reader:
We still have no explanation of the horrible ordeal. What happened? However, I now know that we're in her home.

Story:
Sunburned and bug-bitten, Clements was rescued Thursday, 10 days after she and her husband got lost on the edge of a 6,000-acre cattle ranch near the Apache River. Her 88-year-old husband, the Rev. Thomas O. Clements, died July 14. He suffered from heart disease and used a wheelchair because his diabetes prevented his knees from healing completely after several knee surgeries, she said.

Reader:
Now I'm back where I started. I already know she was

rescued. I already know it was 10 days. I already know it was a ranch. I know her husband died. But how did she and her husband become lost? Were they walking? Was she pushing his wheelchair?

Story:

The Dunbar County Medical Examiner's Office had not released the official cause of death as of yesterday, said Allison Smithson, Clements' daughter-in-law.

Reader:

How did we get to the medical examiner? Why this interruption? Where did Allison come from? What happened to the Clementses?

Story:

Married for seven years, the Coal City couple were returning July 8 from visiting friends and family in Brampton, when Eleanor Clements made a wrong turn onto the Tumbleweed Ranch. A rare rain the night before in the drought-stricken part of the state muddied the dirt road and their van got stuck. Their citizens band radio antenna had been broken by low-hanging branches, Clements said.

Reader:

I'm lost. I thought we were discussing the medical examiner. What's the connection between being married seven years and the visit to friends? At last I know they were in a van. How could the Clementses make a wrong turn? Was it raining? Was it at night? Why did she continue on the dirt road? You said earlier that Eleanor was in a desiccated area. But the van got stuck in the mud. How could she be in a desiccated (which means completely dry) area and get stuck in the mud?

Story:

Hearing faint sounds of distant traffic, she honked the horn and flashed her lights until the battery died.

Reader:

Why didn't she walk back on the dirt road? I guess it was night, because she's flashing lights. How far had they gone, and why?

Story:

With no food, the couple drank two cans of Ensure, a liquid dietary supplement, diet soda that had turned flat in the heat and what water Clements could find, she said.

Reader:

When did all that happen? I thought she was honking the horn and flashing the lights? What day is it?

Story:

She stayed with her husband rather than search for help because without her help, he'd drop the cup. "Water is too valuable to waste it," she said.

Reader:

When did that happen? What day is it? Why must he hold the cup? I'm thoroughly confused. Why didn't she walk down the dirt road toward the traffic sounds?

Story:

"He lasted six days and that's a blessing because he was a sick man," Clements said of her husband, who was founder of House of God Church in Brampton. In 1987, he retired as pastor of Wayside Community Church in Coal City, where he will be buried tomorrow.

Reader:

That's confusing. What was a blessing? That he lasted six days or that he died? Why are you bothering me with details of his life when I want to know about the Clementses' ordeal?

Story:

News reports told of wild hogs in the area, but Clements said her closest animal encounter was with a black bull.

Reader:

What news reports? Was she listening to a radio? Why did the reports mention wild hogs? Why do I need this information now? How did I get to a report on hogs and the sighting of a bull? What's happening to Eleanor and Thomas?

Story:

"He stared at us and we stared at him, and he walked away," she said.

Reader:

Why do I need to know that?

Story:

When the Rev. Clements died on the morning of July 14, she covered his body with a blanket and scattered branches on it to protect it from animals. Then she began to regroup. "I'm not just going to sit in this van and die," she said to herself.

Reader:

Now, I'm back to the ordeal after seeing a bull and hearing wild hog reports. The Rev. Clements dies again. This is the third time you've mentioned it. Why did she cover his body with a blanket and branches? Why didn't she just leave him in the van?

Story:

She began to search for water and help. The only water she found was the dirty and salty rainwater she found in a creek, she said.

Reader:

Now she's searching. Why not earlier? Why didn't she walk down the dirt road toward the traffic sounds? How did we get a creek in a desiccated area?

Story:

While looking for stray cattle, ranch intern Bobby Ray Clampson came across the retired minister's abandoned wheelchair at the northeast end of the Tumbleweed Ranch. Later he found the diary, the van and the dead man's body.

Reader:

I'm confused. You were just talking about Eleanor searching, and now we have a ranch intern finding a wheelchair. How did the wheelchair get out of the van? Where was Eleanor?

Story:

"If the ranch hands hadn't come around, her life could have been gone too," Smithson said.

Reader:

Where are we now? How did we get back to Smithson? What happened to Eleanor? How did they find her?

Story:

In addition to her faith, her routines of walking and

water aerobics "paid off," Clements said.

Reader:
More digression. Why should I be concerned about her faith and exercise? Let's get back to the story.

Story:
"If I hadn't . . . I don't think I would have had the stamina" to survive, she said.

Reader:
I'm confused. She was in great shape, but she couldn't walk to the road where the traffic noise was coming from?

Story:
The diary that she said helped sustain her through the ordeal is still in the custody of the Grump County Sheriff's Department, said Sally Hartson, a jailer.

Reader:
How did we get to the jail? What does the sheriff's department have to do with the story? Isn't what happened to Eleanor more important than what happened to the diary?

Story:
The couple's friends in Coal City were not alarmed by unanswered phone calls because the Clements were "always on the go," Smithson said.

Reader:
How did I get here? When did these friends call? What happened to Eleanor?

Story:
"Assuming someone arrives at their home like they

always do is the wrong thing to do. But you don't know that until later," Smithson said.

Reader:

Who assumed that? The friends? Smithson?

Story:

Smithson, 30, and her husband Rawley, 32, both of Grand Mesa, had met the Clementses in Coal City to visit, Allison Smithson said. Eleanor Clements has three sons. The Rev. Clements had two sons and four daughters, Smithson said.

Reader:

Why do I need to know their ages? Why the family tree? What happened to Eleanor?

Story:

Clements recently quit her job at the Coal City Tribune as a circulation employee to spend more time caring for her husband, she said.

Reader:

What does all that have to do with this story? What's happening to Eleanor?

Story:

"My son said he didn't want to leave me here alone" without a way of getting help in an emergency. I said, 'Don't worry. I'm not going anywhere.' "

Reader:

When did he say that? What happened on the ranch? Is this the end of the story? How could it be? I'm confused.

No wonder the poor reader is confused. The story wanders and is riddled with unanswered questions. It's a story about survival — about a woman's ordeal and rescue. It's a drama, not a news story. It could have been riveting. But it is not. It's disorganized and cluttered. The author has to answer many questions and put the story in order. The writer either has to dig up more information from notes or talk again with Eleanor Clements. Too much information is missing. You should suggest an outline. Here's one possible way to reorganize the story:

Focus:
Woman survives ordeal

Developments:
1. Couple becomes lost
2. Ordeal kills mate
3. Woman fights elements

Ending:
Rescuers find woman

That outline assumes that the author's revised beginning will be similar to the original — with Eleanor Clements safe at home. The story could then tell of her ordeal, ending with the rescue.

However, it could begin when the Clementses left for home, or when they made the wrong turn. Whatever the beginning, the outline would change little. The developments would be similar and the focus would remain Eleanor's survival.

After you've examined the story carefully, made notes on the faulty segments, and suggested ways to revise it, you have to discuss it with the writer or the writer's desk editor. That may mean putting the story off a day or more, but it's a story that will be compelling regardless of the delay. This story's content, not its immediacy, will grab and hold readers. In its present form, the story is not compelling. It's confusing. A patient (and curious) reader may read it to the end, seeking answers to several questions. Most readers won't bother. The writer has to develop Eleanor Clements' ordeal, buttressing both information and emotion.

If the author does not have the necessary information, he or she has to talk again with Eleanor Clements. What did she write in her log? How did they make the wrong turn? How did they become stranded? Why didn't she walk to the main road? What was she thinking during those 10 days? Let her tell the story.

Don't get into the medical examiner, sheriff, and biographical material. That's another story. This story is about a woman surviving a terrifying ordeal. Stick to it.

The outcome, you hope, will be that the writer checks notes, makes phone calls, gets more information, and writes a compelling drama. You've done your job for the moment. You've exercised your reader proxy by voting down a confusing story. You'll have to act for readers again when it comes to fine-tuning the revision.

Exercises

• Find a disorganized news story. Read it, make an outline and revise it. If you find that information is missing, indicate what is needed. Ask a friend who does not work for your company or is not in the journalism department at your school to read the original and comment. Compare your assessment with the independent reader's comments. If there is a big difference, revise your outline and rewrite the story, addressing the reader's comments.

• Find a disorganized feature story of about 750 to 1,000 words. Follow the same procedure you used in the news-story exercise.

Chapter 4

A fresh start:
Repairing story leads

A bad beginning makes a bad ending.
— Euripides

The lead is the beginning of the story. It may be one sentence or several. It must capture the reader's attention, it must capture the essence of the story, and it must provide a smooth transition into the body of the story. A clever lead is useless if it does not do those three things. A good lead is most effective when it moves quickly, using as few words as possible. Author and writing coach Don Murray says, "I have yet to find a good news story — one that really works — with a bad lead." The lead's importance means that writers and editors should probably spend more time on the lead than they do on most other sentences in the story.

But editors should not sit and stare at the terminal, trying to make a lead an award-winner. Try to work with what the writer gave you, and try to help the writer polish it. Don't force the lead. A good lead should come naturally. It should fit the story like an old shoe — comfortably. However, there will be times when the writer's idea cannot be made to work. Rewriting may then be the only solution.

Discuss it with the writer if at all possible.

Leads do not always have to be clever grabbers. There is nothing wrong with a straight news or summary lead — it's strong, to the point and informative. Leads should contain the gist of the story, and that is what readers want.

The feature or delayed lead may not get right to the point, but it often can capture a reader's attention as well as or better than the straight news lead. The feature lead may use anecdotes, mood, irony, metaphor, simile, etc. But word play isn't for every story. Good writers and editors will recognize when a story can carry a feature lead and when it is necessary to play it straight. And they'll make sure the feature lead fits the story. What follows the lead must pick up the thought, mood, essence, etc., of the lead. It cannot go off in another direction.

Make the lead move quickly, using few words and strong words. Remember the reader. French philosopher Blaise Pascal said, "Anything that is written to please the author is worthless." So, try to please the reader. Author John McPhee calls the lead a flashlight shining down into the story. So, beam the reader on to material that flows clearly and logically from the lead.

If you find you're struggling to suggest a better lead, ask the writer some questions:

- •What is the focus of the story — what is it about?
- •What does the reader want to know?
- •How would you begin a conversation about this story?
- •Does anything in the lead affect the reader directly?

Then ask the writer to make a simple outline, noting the key segments of the story. And finally, ask the author to write one sentence that says what the story is about. That sentence may even turn out to be the lead. If not, it will certainly provide a good start toward writing a strong, captivating lead. Of course, if the author is not present or can't be reached in a reasonable time, you'll have to revise the lead or delay the story.

When suggesting revision, don't force your own style or voice on the story. Also don't be frightened when a writer tries something different. Encourage reasonable experimentation. Writers learn by trying new words, structures, styles, etc. As long as it's clear and easy to read, try it. If you've produced a bomb, your colleagues and readers will let you know. And you and the writer will have learned something by trying. Keep in mind when experimenting that natural leads work best — those that are conversational and not forced.

A writer I worked with early in my career kept a journal of lead ideas. Whenever a clever lead came to mind, he'd write it in his journal. He had quite a few pages of "leads," and shared them with me. Some were good, just waiting for a story to go with them. Others were clichés. I remembered one in particular, and I used it years later when I was writing sports. It was "What can you say after you've said you're sorry?" I had covered a high school football game and the score was lopsided, something like 60 to 0. On the way back to the office, I thought of that lead and used it on that game story. It seemed appropriate, but I always felt a little ashamed for writing it. It wasn't mine, and it was trite.

That lead was not fresh or conversational, and perhaps would have benefited from an editor's counseling. Leads like that, or some version of it, are not uncommon. The cliché lead does not necessarily employ a cliché. It relies on formula writing. Mostly, it's stale.

Several years ago, two colleagues had been talking about formula leads, citing examples of some that they had read and possible versions of them. They compiled a list and shared it with me. Years later, I added some of my own examples to it. Here are some common cliché leads, including the versions of the original examples. However, it's by no means a complete list. I'm sure you can add some of your own.

■ The Webster's Dictionary lead

Webster's defines cliché as a trite phrase or expression. If that's true, then this lead is a cliché, and . . . .

■ The "that's what" lead

Some leads are easier to write than others. That's what 15 journalists participating in copy-editing seminar said Monday.

■ The faulty "Fred Zimmerman" lead

Fred Zimmerman reached into his rear pants pocket and pulled out his worn brown leather wallet. He fumbled through the small denomination bills, crumpled grocery lists, credit cards and old photographs before pulling out a shiny new card with his picture on the front.

Zimmerman is one of many who have opted for the new photo ID credit cards.

■ The "What's My Line" lead

It's new. It's state of the art. It's easy to use, and even easier to understand. It's the new online classroom.

■ The common question lead

What do Charlie Chaplin and Bill Clinton have in common?

■ The "exceptional" lead

Most journalists have trouble writing a snappy lead, and Edgar Poo is no exception.

■ The go-look-it-up lead

When Paul LaRocque was born, Franklin D. Roosevelt was president and newspapers cost less than a nickel.

■ The one-word lead (A variation of the "that's what" lead)

Cynical.
That's what most people think journalists are.

■ The word lead (A variation of the "one-word" lead)

Flabbergasted was the only word the workshop instructor could think of when all the writers got their orientation exercises done on time.

■ The holiday lead

Today is Valentine's Day, but you wouldn't know it by the way taxi drivers are treating their riders.

■ The Rodney Dangerfield lead

Garbage collectors get no respect.
Lawyers get no respect.
But coach Blackie Schwartz says his Cyclones are going to get respect.

■ The "typical" lead

At first glance, the Associated Press Managing Editors seems to be just another journalism organization. It's that and more, says Caesar Andrews, APME president.

■ The I-fooled-you lead

Sex, drugs and booze.
That's not what you'll find in newsrooms today, said Kent Clark, managing editor of the Gotham Daily Planet.

■ The question lead

Ever wonder what happened to Tom Mix?
Most people don't. The famous movie cowboy of yesterday is not a familiar name among today's moviegoers. But ask a teen-ager about Brad Pitt, and you'll get a complete biography.

■ The "many" lead

Many journalists don't know they exist, but online courses in newspapering are being offered by several universities.

■ The time-is-important lead

Today, September 22, is the first day of online instruction for journalists across the country.

■ The that's good, that's bad lead

The good news is that on-line classes have begun.
The bad news is that most students don't have computers.

■ The now-look-at lead

When your parents bought their first home, mortgage interest rates were only 2 percent. Now look at what they are.

■ The quote lead

"It was a wonderful contest, and I'm glad my pie won,"
said Jessica Pillsbury upon getting her blue ribbon at the
Whoopee County Fair Saturday.

Generally, avoid the cliché lead. However, there may be a rare time when a cliché lead or a version of it is the best choice. Be fresh, but be flexible.

The most common and most annoying cliché lead is the faulty "people" lead. Journalists, looking for a label for such leads, called them Fred Zimmerman leads. The name stuck. Zimmerman leads are anecdotal, using people doing something that is related to the story's theme. Properly employed, a Zimmerman lead can be compelling, interesting, and a readable way to begin a story. Like a good wine, a good Zimmerman can delight the senses and brighten a story. But too much can make your head spin. Some newspaper journalists, thinking that people are much more interesting than facts and figures, tend to overwork Mr. Zimmerman. Good writing does not force narrative where it is inappropriate, such as leading a straight news item with a Zimmerman.

However, when used correctly, as in the first two leads below, the Zimmerman can be effective. The first, by Peter Landers of The Associated Press, sets up the scene so the reader knows right away what the story is about and why the scene is relevant. The second gives us the scene and foreshadows the relevance.

The dainty Japanese appetite is growing. One need only peek in on the all-you-can-eat restaurants that have become Japan's newest dining trend.

Atsuko Unozawa can't get enough.

"Whenever I come here, I try to eat one more

piece than I had the last time," said the only slightly pudgy 24-year-old woman during a recent visit to the Cheesecake Factory in Tokyo.

Total consumption: 12 slices.

From cheesecake to sushi, Chinese food to Italian, Japanese are filling up at restaurants that offer as much food as they can possibly ingest in a sitting for a single, moderate price. At the Cheesecake Factory, that is $15.

Big-eating Japanese-style is known as "Viking," a reference to a restaurant that pioneered the all-you-can-eat concept in Japan, the now-closed Imperial Viking. The restaurant itself took its name from an old Kirk Douglas movie called "The Vikings" that depicted marauding — and presumably big-eating — Scandinavians.

Perhaps the Imperial Viking was ahead of its time when it opened in the 1950s.

No more. In the past five years, the popularity of all-you-can-eat restaurants has exploded.

This Zimmerman lead foreshadows the theme:

The mother of the bride dabbed her eyes, the other guests spluttered and even the registrar burst out laughing when Joanne married Paul on a recent sunny autumn day.

The reason? Tucked between the solemn couple, head on hand in the manner of a weary judge, stood their 4-year-old son, Ben.

The scene may not be lifted from "Four Weddings and a Funeral," but then, this is real life, and in real-life Britain today the typical wedding involves a man and woman near or past 30, who often are tying the knot long after the birth of their first child.

If, that is, if they marry at all.

In a growing swathe of British society, the traditional family has disappeared — replaced by unmarried "partners," indefinite cohabitation and children born out of wedlock.

When the Zimmerman is not used wisely, as in the lead below, it can be ridiculous.

Charlotte Myers put down the rag she had been using to wipe the counter, put her hands on her hips and exhaled a small, exasperated sigh. It was another day of Government gridlock, and the news out of Washington, playing on the television set above the bar, called for more of the same.

"I just don't think it's right," she said.

"It's going to hurt too many people, and soon it's going to hurt us all."

"My husband's on Social Security and on Medicare," Ms. Myers, the bartender at Kinzer's Station Tavern, went on, resuming her wiping. "It's scary."

By now Americans are certainly no strangers to political brinkmanship. Practically every year, it seems, Congress and the President pitch the Government into another self-inflicted crisis.

But if people in this part of the country are any gauge, it seems that this time Americans are taking the showdown in Washington with a concern that edges toward alarm.

There is nothing wrong with trying to humanize a story by pulling into its lead at least one person who can symbolize the theme. It's a way of reducing macrocosm to microcosm. It's a good technique when it works, but too often it doesn't work. The Zimmerman will work only if we find the right person to represent the macrocosm. That person must not only do the right things, he or she must do interesting things that are related to the story's theme. That's a principle of good fiction writing, and it should be a principle of good nonfiction as well. We want people to read our stories. And perhaps even more important, we want them to discover something.

The New York Times' Max Frankel tells us: "If an anecdote leads a report of major significance, it bears a heavy obligation to busy readers to encapsulate the very essence of the report" (From "Word & Image: Scene but Not Heard," Sunday, May 10, 1998).

Here's a comment on Zimmerman leads that a reporter made in one of my writing seminars:

"The concept of Zimmermans is intriguing to me. A lot of newspapers apparently instruct their reporters to produce these kinds of leads. An acquaintance who works at a newspaper in Florida says her editors have instructed that every single story have such a lead. I think it's part of the hyper-localization of news: the thinking that readers don't care unless the story affects someone just like them."

Let's fix a few leads. Here are the leads, first in their original form and next with my comments. Again, you might want to mark the original as you read it and compare your comments with mine.

Example 1

Omaha, Neb. — A 28-year veteran of the Nebraska State Patrol has been charged with two counts of theft in connection with cases in Stanton and Madison counties, a special prosecutor said Friday.

Dodge County Attorney Dean Skokan, who was

named special prosecutor by Madison County Attorney Joe Smith, said Patrolman Gunther Getter was charged with one count of felony theft by unlawful taking in Stanton County and one count of receiving stolen property in Madison County.

Skokan said arraignments have been scheduled for 11 a.m. July 12 in Madison County and 1 p.m. the same day in Stanton County.

Let's put on our reader hats and comment.

Story:
Omaha, Neb. — A 28-year veteran of the Nebraska State Patrol has been charged with two counts of theft in connection with cases in Stanton and Madison counties, a special prosecutor said Friday.

Reader:
Not bad. The first sentence gets right to the subject. Who is this guy and what did he do?

Story:
Dodge County Attorney Dean Skokan, who was named special prosecutor by Madison County Attorney Joe Smith, said Patrolman Gunther Getter was charged with one count of felony theft by unlawful taking in Stanton County and one count of receiving stolen property in Madison County.

Reader:
Why do you tell me who the special prosecutor is and who appointed him before you tell me the officer's name? And you repeat information that was in the first sentence. Also, the first sentence says he has been charged with two counts of theft, but the next sentence says one count of theft and one of receiving stolen property.

Story:

Skokan said arraignments have been scheduled for 11 a.m. July 12 in Madison County and 1 p.m. the same day in Stanton County.

Reader:

Thanks. I was just going to ask about that.

Now, you're the editor again. How are you going to help the reader? Here's one way you can edit this lead (new wording is in italic type):

Omaha, Neb. — A 28-year veteran of the Nebraska State Patrol has been charged with ~~two counts of~~ theft. ~~in connection with cases in Stanton and Madison counties, a special prosecutor said Friday. Dodge County Attorney Dean Skokan, who was named special prosecutor by Madison County Attorney Joe Smith, said~~ Patrolman Gunther Getter ~~was charged with~~ *faces* one count of felony theft ~~by unlawful taking~~ in Stanton County and one count of receiving stolen property in Madison County, a special prosecutor said Friday.

Dodge County Attorney Dean Skokan, who was appointed special prosecutor by Madison County Attorney Joe Smith, ~~Skokan~~ said arraignments ~~have~~ *had* been scheduled for 11 a.m. July 12 in Madison County and 1 p.m. the same day in Stanton County.

This edited lead cuts 14 words — from 97 words to 83. And it moves quickly through the important information, saving the official details for later. Here's the finished story.

Omaha, Neb. — A 28-year veteran of the Nebraska State Patrol has been charged with theft. Patrolman Gunther Getter faces one count of felony theft in Stanton County and one count of receiving

stolen property in Madison County, a special prosecutor said Friday.

Dodge County Attorney Dean Skokan, who was
appointed special prosecutor by Madison County
Attorney Joe Smith, said arraignments had been
scheduled for 11 a.m. July 12 in Madison County
and 1 p.m. the same day in Stanton County.

That news lead required quite a bit of tightening. Now
let's look at a different situation — a feature story marking the anniversary of a famous plane crash. It's a
Zimmerman. What does it need? Remember, read first as
a reader. Make comments if you wish and compare them
to the marked version that follows.

Example 2

Easter Heathman bent his neck and began to
search the prairie at his feet. The kind of wind that
makes a man hunch his shoulders blew noisily from
the west. Behind Heathman stood a 10-foot-high
stone monument. Beyond the memorial, the Flint
Hills, still wearing their dun winter coats, rose and
dipped to the horizon.

Heathman, 73, spied the object of his search
and plucked it from a damp patch of dirt.

"You can still find pieces of glass from the
cracked windshield," he said. "Somebody thought
maybe this glass was from a pop bottle. It's all the
same thickness. If it were from a bottle, some would
be curved, some straight."

Four chunks of glass are found, the biggest of
which is as thick as two quarters. They are slivers
of history, like Minie balls discovered on a Civil
War battleground. Gettysburg didn't ask to be a historic site. Fate and death anointed it. So it is with

this crest of rolling pasture.

At 10:47 a.m. on Tuesday, March 31, 1931 – 60 years ago Sunday – a Fokker F-10 passenger plane dived out of a leaden sky and buried itself into this piece of Kansas. The two pilots and six passengers on Transcontinental & Western Air Express Flight 599 perished instantly, which is also how quickly the news spread across the nation.

One of the passengers had been Notre Dame football coach Knute Rockne.

Put on the reader hat, and we'll comment.

Story:

Easter Heathman bent his neck and began to search the prairie at his feet. The kind of wind that makes a man hunch his shoulders blew noisily from the west. Behind Heathman stood a 10-foot-high stone monument. Beyond the memorial, the Flint Hills, still wearing their dun winter coats, rose and dipped to the horizon.

Reader:

What's happening? What is Heathman looking for? Is he lost? Where is he? Why should I read more?

Story:

Heathman, 73, spied the object of his search and plucked it from a damp patch of dirt.

Reader:

What did he find? Why is his age important?

Story:

"You can still find pieces of glass from the cracked windshield," he said. "Somebody thought maybe this glass was from a pop bottle. It's all the same thickness. If it were from a bottle, some would be curved, some straight."

Reader:

Again, what's happening? Is he at the site of an automobile accident? So it doesn't look like glass from a pop bottle. So what.

Story:

Four chunks of glass are found, the biggest of which is as thick as two quarters. They are slivers of history, like Minie balls discovered on a Civil War battleground. Gettysburg didn't ask to be a historic site. Fate and death anointed it. So it is with this crest of rolling pasture.

Reader:

What does the battle of Gettysburg have to do with this? Where are we? What history?

Story:

At 10:47 a.m. on Tuesday, March 31, 1931 – 60 years ago Sunday – a Fokker F-10 passenger plane dived out of a leaden sky and buried itself into this piece of Kansas. The two pilots and six passengers on Transcontinental & Western Air Express Flight 599 perished instantly, which is also how quickly the news spread across the nation.

Reader:

Oh my gosh. So that's what happened, and we're in Kansas. But why is that crash historic?

Story:

One of the passengers had been Notre Dame football coach Knute Rockne.

Reader:

At last, I have the answer. It was the plane crash that

killed Knute Rockne. Why didn't you tell me that earlier? I had no idea this story was about the anniversary of his death until that last sentence.

That's a lead that should go back to the author. It's greatly overwritten. The Zimmerman lead can work, but it has to provide some hint of the story's focus — well before the sixth paragraph. There's no one way to revise that lead. However, it does need revision. Here are two revision examples — one keeps the Zimmerman lead and is much tighter, the other is more direct but retains much of the original's information. Both are revisions written by participants in workshops that I conducted. And both are better than the original — the first because it's compact and lets readers know what the story is about, the second because it's direct. (Although the second example gets directly into the story, it still suffers from overwriting. We'll revisit those examples in Chapter 5 when we discuss compression.)

The original lead offers no hint of the story's focus — the anniversary of the death of Knute Rockne. Instead, we have diversions in the form of weather, scenery, age, history, etc.

The first revision keeps Heathman in the lead but gives readers strong hints about the story — glass and history. The second paragraph answers the questions those two items raised — the plane crash that killed Rockne.

The second revision gets directly to the focus — the anniversary of a plane crash in the first sentence and the reason (Rockne's death) it's remembered in the second sentence.

The original does not do the three things essential for good leads. It does not grab reader attention, does not include the essence of the story, and does not move smoothly and quickly into the story.

Revision No. 1

Easter Heathman scraped a patch of dusty prairie and picked up four small objects – chunks of glass, slivers of history.

"You can still find pieces of glass from the cracked windshield," Heathman said, referring to the plane that crashed there 60 years ago Sunday. The plane, Transcontinental & Western Air Express Flight 599, plunged from a leaden Kansas sky into that piece of prairie, killing Notre Dame football coach Knute Rockne and seven others.

Revision No. 2

Sixty years ago a small plane dived out of a leaden sky and buried itself in this piece of Kansas.

Today, a stone monument towers over the crash site where Notre Dame football coach Knute Rockne and seven other passengers died in the shadow of the Flint Hills.

Anointed by fate and death, this crest of rolling pasture has become a historic site.

And decades after the accident, the curious still flock to the area to hunt for remnants of the disaster.

Easter Heathman is one of them. Hunching his shoulders to the force of the howling wind, Heathman, 73, inspects the earth at his feet.

His search uncovers four chunks of glass from the plane's cracked windshield — slivers of history like Minie balls discovered on a Civil War battleground.

Next, let's look at a news lead disguised as a feature — with a Zimmerman lead.

Go through it first as a reader, making notes that you can compare with my comments when we look at the story again.

Example 3

When it comes to shopping at The Parks at Arlington mall, Jackie Schley knows where the back roads are.

"I've lived here a while, so I know how to get around through Matlock [Road] and Arbrook [Boulevard]," said Ms. Schley, a southeast Arlington resident. "I avoid the Cooper [Street] and Interstate 20 intersection at all costs."

In about two years, more people will be able to avoid that busy intersection.

Some 57,000 vehicles travel north and south on Cooper every day at I-20 — about 22,000 more than it was originally designed to hold, according to city estimates. The traffic increases significantly beyond that during the busy Christmas shopping season, which starts next month.

Another 140,000 vehicles travel east and west along I-20 daily at Cooper.

A $4.5 million project — to reverse exit and entrance ramps on the north side of I-20 between Cooper and Matlock and overlay the frontage roads — is slated to start next April and be complete by September 2001.

"The ramp reversal will be one of the most significant projects to reduce congestion at Cooper and I-20 that we can do," said Michael Hasler, the city's director of transportation.

The City Council on Tuesday approved adding $29,500 to the design of the project, increasing Arlington-based Graham Associates' contract to

$289,500. The contract was originally approved in March.

The extra money is needed because the Texas Department of Transportation determined that the proposed asphalt for the overlay was not adequate to carry the projected traffic and that ten inches of concrete was needed, said Allen Harts, a municipal civil engineer.

Put your reader hat back on, and let's compare your notes to mine.

Story:

When it comes to shopping at The Parks at Arlington mall, Jackie Schley knows where the back roads are.

Reader:

Why should I care? Who's she?

Story:

"I've lived here a while, so I know how to get around through Matlock [Road] and Arbrook [Boulevard]," said Ms. Schley, a southeast Arlington resident. "I avoid the Cooper [Street] and Interstate 20 intersection at all costs."

Reader:

So what? Who is she, and why should I care that she knows the "back roads." Why should I be concerned?

Story:

In about two years, more people will be able to avoid that busy intersection.

Reader:

What's happening in two years? Where did Jackie go? What's this story about?

Story:

Some 57,000 vehicles travel north and south on Cooper every day at I-20 — about 22,000 more than it was originally designed to hold, according to city estimates. The traffic increases significantly beyond that during the busy Christmas shopping season, which starts next month.

Reader:

Oh! I guess this is a traffic story. What's going to happen in two years?

Story:

Another 140,000 vehicles travel east and west along I-20 daily at Cooper.

Reader:

More traffic figures. That's a busy area, but what's happening in two years?

Story:

A $4.5 million project — to reverse exit and entrance ramps on the north side of I-20 between Cooper and Matlock and overlay the frontage roads — is slated to start next April and be complete by September 2001.

Reader:

Ah, that's it. The intersection is going to be improved. Why didn't you say that?

Story:

"The ramp reversal will be one of the most significant projects to reduce congestion at Cooper and I-20 that we can do," said Michael Hasler, the city's director of transportation.

Reader:

That's nice, but what will happen when the ramps are reversed? What does that mean?

Story:

The City Council on Tuesday approved adding $29,500 to the design of the project, increasing Arlington-based Graham Associates' contract to $289,500. The contract was originally approved in March.

Reader:

Well, that's the news. The city is changing the design contract. I had to read seven paragraphs before you told me why I should be interested in this story. Instead of all those wasted words, you could have told me about the changes in the project.

Story:

The extra money is needed because the Texas Department of Transportation determined that the proposed asphalt for the overlay was not adequate to carry the projected traffic and that ten inches of concrete was needed, said Allen Harts, a municipal civil engineer.

Reader:

Fine. More base is needed in the road. Get on with the details.

That lead can be repaired easily by the editor. All that's needed is to cut out Jackie Schley, begin with the council action, and then move to the changes in the project. The story has other problems, but we'll deal here only with the structure. Here's how it might look:

The City Council has approved an increase in funding for the design of interchange improvements at Interstate 20 and Cooper Street, which is scheduled to start in April.

An additional $29,500 was needed to meet state standards. The Texas Department of Transportation said the asphalt surface should be replaced with 10 inches of concrete in order to support the traffic that the roads will carry.

The original design contract for $289,500 with Graham Associates of Arlington was approved in March.

Let's look next at a quick-fix lead, one that tosses out several numbers, which slow readers and are unnecessary in the lead. Numbers often are important to the story and should sometimes be in the lead — budget stories, storm or accident casualties, etc. But too many numbers hinder readability. Three numbers is a fair limit in most sentences, but that may be too many for a lead sentence. Consider the following sentence. It has five numbers, most of which are unnecessary. Put the important figures in the lead sentence. You have the rest of the story to display the other numbers, if necessary.

Example 4

Eldon George, now 26, who in 1985 pleaded guilty to the murder of 56-year-old Maria Angel, has been paroled after serving 10 years of his 50-year sentence.

You don't need the victim's age in the lead. Get to that later. The year is not important here. It can wait until later in the story. Inclusion of George's present age is not as significant as his age when the crime was committed. The sentence time is important. That leaves you with three numbers — age at the time of the crime, years he served, and sentence. Here's a suggested revision:

> Eldon George, who pleaded guilty to murdering a woman when he was 16, has been paroled after serving 10 years of a 50-year sentence.

Exercises

• Look through several publications and find five cliché leads. Are they appropriate for the stories they lead? Explain your response. If the leads are not appropriate, rewrite them so they are reader friendly.

• Find a Zimmerman lead that works and explain why it works.

• Find a Zimmerman lead that does not work and explain why it doesn't. Rewrite it, either keeping the Zimmerman or eliminating it. Make your revised lead reader friendly.

Chapter 5

Tighter, please:
Pruning, compressing, and strengthening

He has a genius for compressing a minimum of ideas into a maximum of words.
— Winston Churchill

Compressed writing, like the disciplined athlete, is slimmer and stronger. It's writing with muscle. Editors are language body builders. They should not only work off unnecessary words, but should rebuild weak passages with strong words. In this chapter, you'll get some suggestions for keeping fit with words.

Sometimes the need for pruning writing is obvious. If you run short of breath reading a sentence, you probably need to get rid of some words or break one sentence into two or more. Often, the need for pruning may not be obvious. A sentence can be a reasonable length but flabby. You can make it stronger by replacing a weak verb with a strong one, restructuring it to get rid of a few prepositions, replacing abstract language with concrete words, changing the sentence from passive to active voice, etc. The sentence you just read has 39 words, but it's not difficult to read — perhaps because it's a list. The list items concern one topic — improving readability — which gives them unity. Use sentence length as a guide, not as a rule. The chief consideration for any sentence is readability. Consider this opening passage from Herman Melville's *Moby Dick*.

> *Call me Ishmael. Some years ago — never mind how long precisely — having little or no money in my purse, and nothing particular to interest me on shore, I thought I would sail about a little and see the watery part of the world. It is a way I have of driving off the spleen, and regulating the circulation. Whenever I find myself growing grim about the mouth; whenever it is a damp, drizzly November in my soul; whenever I find myself involuntarily pausing before coffin warehouses, and bringing up the rear of every funeral I meet; and especially whenever my hypos get such an upper hand of me, that it requires a strong moral principle to prevent me from deliberately stepping into the street, and methodically knocking people's hats off — then, I account it high time to get to sea as soon as I can.*

The passage glides on a rhythm of sentences, repetition, and parallel structure — three words, 40, 15, and then 87 words. The long last sentence is helped by semicolon breaks, parallel structure, repetition, and a short list of the moods that say it's time to "get to sea." That passage is not difficult reading. But it's built on a whopper sentence of 87 words. Repeating *whenever* and the parallel structure of those clauses — *whenever I find, whenever I find, whenever my* — builds to a conclusion of similar structure — *then, I account*. Rebuilding that passage would surely harm its rhythm and mood. Editors should not merely count words. They should *read* them before attempting surgery. If the words float by like notes of a catchy song, then let them float — as long as they are pleasing. It's the sour and monotonous notes that need an editor's touch.

Varying sentence length can give rhythm to writing. And long sentences with rhythm often can be clearer and more pleasing than short sentences without rhythm.

As you can see, there is no magic number for sentence length. But if a sentence is longer than 25 words, consider using a period or two. The emphasis is on *consider*. A sentence that is too long will cry, "stop me." Read it aloud, and you'll hear the cry.

Sentences are sometimes difficult to read not only because they have too many words, but because they contain unnecessary and unclear words. The meaning of a sentence should be clear in one reading. If you have to reread a sentence, that's a good sign that it needs repair.

Readability indexes can be helpful in determining whether a passage is concise, but they are merely statistical measures. A good index score does not guarantee readability. Some word processing applications include readability indexes in their spelling- and grammar-check programs. Those indexes are quick gauges that focus primarily on sentence length and the number of syllables in words. Use them as reference if you have time, but rely chiefly on your reader sense to tell you whether a sentence, passage, or story is difficult reading.

For example, the Flesch Index, developed by Rudolf Flesch, gives the Melville passage above a 55.1 score, which translates to *fairly difficult* reading. The Flesch index uses words per sentence and syllables per 100 words to measure readability. The scale is 0 to 100, with 100 being the most readable. A Flesch score between 60 and 70 is considered standard reading ease. With Flesch's index, the higher the score, the better.

The Fog Index, developed by Robert Gunning, uses grade level as a gauge of readability. Melville gets a bit more than 17 on the Fog Index, which means it's at college graduate school reading level. Gunning also counts sentence length and syllables in "difficult" words — words of three or more syllables. A score of 10, for example, would mean the writing is at the 10th-grade level. Most popular magazines are written at that level, Gunning says. With Gunning's index, the lower the score, the better.

Editors would be misled if they compressed the Melville passage on the basis of a readability score. However, the index scores on the following passage provide a strong hint that something is wrong. The writer attempts to squeeze too much into one sentence, includes unnecessary long words, and uses a weak verb to carry the main action. Sentences such as this can exhaust readers, and they should be edited.

> Parents whose children will attend Nichols Junior High School next year have the opportunity to vote this week on a referendum that would implement the school district's first mandatory uniform policy.
>
> (One sentence, 31 words, a Fog Index of 20, and a Flesch index of 23.6.)

Here's an easy way to repair faulty sentences. Start with the basics. Find the main action in the sentence. Then find the actor and the receiver, if there is one. You will then have an active-voice skeleton — subject-verb-object. Let's try that with this sentence.

The main action is *vote*. The actor is *parents*. There is no direct object because *vote* is an intransitive verb. The indirect object is the phrase *on whether their children must wear uniforms*. Thus *parents vote on uniforms* is the skeleton. Now, simply add the necessary modifiers, and you have a complete and tight sentence. Add the important qualifier — *the first district school* — in a second sentence and you have this passage:

> Parents of students attending Nichols Junior High School next year will vote this week on whether their children must wear uniforms. If parents approve, Nichols will be the first district school to require uniforms.
>
> (Two sentences, 34 words, 9.1 Fog Index, and a Flesch Index of 60.1.)

Note that *mandatory uniform policy* becomes *must wear uniforms* — active verbs and simple words opposed to a mouthful of abstract nouns. And you've done away with wordy combinations such as *have the opportunity to vote on* and *a referendum that would implement.*

The action in that passage is easy to find. It is a verb. Sometimes, however, the action may be disguised as a noun or other part of speech, such as in this sentence. *Parents will make a decision on whether their children will have to wear uniforms to school* . . . .The action is *decide*, disguised in that sentence as a noun, *decision.*

One idea

Another way to tighten writing is to limit sentences to one idea. That not only helps keep sentences short, it makes sentences easier for readers to digest. Again, there will be exceptions — sentences in which two or more independent clauses easily link ideas, lengthy sentences that present a readable list of items, and sentences with rhythmic devices such as parallel structure and repetition. The first sentence below has at least three major ideas, and it is 61 words. Try reading it without pausing for a breath. You can't do it. Editors can recognize overweight sentences simply by their bulk, but the true test of weight is in the reading.

But there is a new legend in the making these days for the rank-and-file of the International Brotherhood of Teamsters, and its unlikely hero is a 55-year-old former United Parcel Service driver who, after 23 years leading an obscure local in New York City, has just been elected to a five-year term as president of the 1.5-million member international union.

His name is Ronald Carey, and they say he is an honest man.

Here's an easier-to-read version. It's broken into three sentences, each with one topic.

But the International Brotherhood of Teamsters rank-and-file has a new a legend in the making. The unlikely hero is a 55-year-old former United Parcel Service driver who has led an obscure New York City local for 23 years. He's Ronald Carey, whom the teamsters have just elected to a five-year term as president of the 1.5-million member international union.

The following descriptive sentence, by the AP's Saul Pett, is also long — 65 words. You won't be able to read it without pausing for a breath, but its rhythmic structure and list of personality traits help make easy reading of this description of former New York Mayor Ed Koch:

He is the freshest thing to blossom in New York since chopped liver, a mixed metaphor of a politician, the antithesis of the packaged leader, irrepressible, candid, impolitic, spontaneous, funny feisty, independent, uncowed by voter blocs, unsexy, unhandsome, unfashionable and altogether charismatic, a man oddly at peace with himself in an unpeaceful place, a mayor who presides over the country's largest Babel with unseemly joy.

Limit prepositions

As you have seen, sentence length affects readability, but not always. Excess of anything is generally not good. For example, too many prepositional phrases in a sentence can affect readability. Prepositions such as *in, of, with, by,* and *for* are valuable little words. But writers sometimes overwork them. Stacking modifying prepositional phrases can make writing sing-song and can create misplaced modifiers. More than three prepositional phrases in a sentence is a good sign that repairs are needed. Note how breaking up the preposition gang helps the following sentence.

> After signatures are turned in and verified by the principal and the school's plan is approved by Mrs. Hale, schools must hold public forums and a referendum for parents to vote on for five consecutive school days. (37 words, five prepositional phrases.)

Right away, you can see that the sentence has problems — it backs in with a prepositional phrase, which is followed by two passive verbs — *are turned in* and *is approved.* And the sentence contains three topics — official approval, school action, and voting. Begin with the subjects instead of backing in with a subordinate phrase, switch to the active voice, and create a new sentence for each of the three topics. The result:

> First, the principal must verify signatures, and Mrs. Hale must approve the school's plan. Next, the

school must hold public forums and an election. Then, parents will have five days in which to vote. (34 words, one prepositional phrase.)

By not backing in you got rid of *after*. By changing from passive to active voice, you got rid of two *by*'s. You dropped *for* twice by breaking the last part of the sentence into two sentences — one concerning forums and election and one about the voting. And you establish easy flow from sentence to sentence with the transitional words *first*, *next*, and *then*.

The next sentence illustrates how stacking prepositions can produce an annoying sing-song rhythm. By the time readers get to Drummond's quote, they have waded through eight prepositional phrases, and they don't care what he has to say. The sentence has rhythm, but it's a cloying rhythm.

David Drummond, one of the three law enforcement officers acquitted in the drowning deaths of three black youths here, stood by his pickup Monday at his home by the railroad tracks in Groesbeck and slowly, in a voice void of emotion, said, "It feels good."

It's got rhythm — too much of it. All those prepositional phrases that pinpoint his location are not only sing-song, they are unnecessary. The focus of that sentence is acquittal and lack of emotion. The rest gets in the way. Find another place for Drummond's truck, home, and railroad tracks — if they are essential to the story.

Here's a sentence in which preposition excess is misleading:

Police found the suspect hiding in a stall in the barn behind a horse with blood on his jacket.

Obviously, the horse was not wearing a bloody jacket, as this sentence might lead readers to believe. Place prepositional phrases next to the words they modify. In this case, the phrase *with blood on his jacket* should follow *suspect*, or it could be in a separate sentence. Here are two revisions:

> Police found the suspect, with blood on his jacket, hiding behind a horse in a barn stall.

> Police found the suspect hiding behind a horse in a barn stall. He had blood on his jacket.

Prefer active voice

When you changed the voice from passive to active in the school-vote sentence above, you made the sentence tighter and stronger. Active voice is conversational. It's natural. A child does not run home from the playground shouting: *I was hit by Johnny*. He cries, *Johnny hit me*. An active-voice verb is stronger — it stands alone. And an active sentence is shorter. You cut out the auxiliary verb *was* and the proposition *by*.

However, passive is not the bad voice that some pedants would have us believe. You can use the passive voice effectively when the actor is not important or unknown: *Bill Clinton was re-elected president. The ship's cargo was damaged sometime during the long voyage.* In the first sentence, the actor — voters — is not important. Who was elected is. In the second sentence, the actor is unknown. You don't know who damaged the cargo.

Fear of passive voice is so strong in some writers that they sometimes see it where it isn't. Passive sentences always contain an auxiliary verb and a past participle. But not all sentences with auxiliary verbs are passive. The passive voice can't be identified solely by whether the sentence employs a form of the verb *to be* as an auxiliary.

Obviously, all sentences with forms of *to be* — *is, are, was, were, be, been, being,* or *am* — are not passive.

Here's an easy way to identify passive sentences: the receiver of the action is in the subject position, the verb consists of a form of the verb *to be,* or sometimes *get,* followed by a past participle. The following sentences are not passive:

The boys were angry. (*Were* links *boys,* the subject, with *angry,* the predicate adjective.)

The girls were walking along the highway. (In this sentence, *were* is an auxiliary verb with the present participle *walking.*)

The following sentence is passive:

The scheme was discovered by police in early August.

Now it's active:

Police discovered the scheme in early August.

Avoid jargon

Active voice gets part of its strength from its conversational tone. Conversational tone does not mean "street talk," and it especially does not mean using jargon, clichés, fad words, and journalese. Those are tired words that often come from the mouths of law enforcement officers, educators, businessmen, government bureaucrats, and too often from the keyboards of journalists. Such language fits easily in formula writing, but it is not conversational. It's dull, tired, and vague. And editors should be wary of it.

How would you react if a friend began a conversation

like this:

"Amid a flurry of activity over a heated debate, my wife left me in a surprise move, which unleashed a new round of difficulties."

You'd probably run quickly to find his wife and congratulate her for leaving the guy.

Every occupation, sport, hobby, etc., has jargon. Journalists use jargon — *head, lead, nut graph,* etc. Jargon sometimes breaks out of its user group and becomes fad expression. Fad words may become clichés by overuse. All those categories contribute to a larger word family called journalese — the jargon, fad words, and clichés so often used by news media that they have become easy devices for satirists and parodies.

Jargon, if used often enough, may become standard language usage. Language is a growing thing. It changes as our world changes. The space program and the personal computer have given us jargon that has filtered into every-day use: *blast off, go into orbit, A-OK, boot up, download, e-mail,* etc. That jargon is useful. Those words function well in our language. However, others are tired and abstract — *scenario, bottom line, bizarre twist, chilling effect, cautiously optimistic, venue,* etc. Avoid such worn-out words. Writing clarity demands fresh and specific words.

But don't be too quick to challenge the cliché just because it is a cliché. Good writers may use clichés because they are the right words for the moment. Or they can manipulate them into something fresh.

A writer, for example, twists a cliché to describe singer Julio Iglesias as an "oil-soaked lounge iguana." Substituting *iguana* recycles and freshens the cliché and plays off the singer's Latin American heritage.

William Safire, writing about Donald Trump, freshens financial jargon when he writes: "The nation's most celebrated deal artist is working on a leveraged throwout of his wife, who betrayed his trust by turning 40."

The *National Review* uses a creative cliché to describe conservative presidential candidate Jack Kemp as the "great right hope."

Use fewer numbers

Numbers, unlike clichés, are generally specific, but they should be used in moderate servings. Some stories, such as those dealing with statistics, budgets, grants, annual reports, etc., are built on numbers. A little extra effort when writing numbers can make stories easier for readers. Pair related figures and do the math for readers when necessary. In comparisons, avoid mixing raw numbers and percentages. Use bulleted lists instead of stacking several figures in a sentence.

This sentence makes the reader work to find the breakdown of student financial aid:

Student financial aid climbed 7.9 percent last year to a record $30.8 billion, with students receiving $15.1 billion in grants, $14.9 billion in loans, and $791 million in work-study earnings.

Break out the figures in a list and it's easy reading.

Student aid increased 7.9 percent last year to a record $30.8 billion. Overall, students received:
• $15.1 billion in grants.
• $14.9 billion in loans.
• $791 million in work-study earnings.

Numbers in leads should be limited. (See the example in Chapter 4.) Leads should move quickly, and only the most important numbers are worthy of a story's first sentence — generally one figure, sometimes two for comparison, but never more than three.

Short is strong

The Fog Index considers words of three or more sylla-bles to be *difficult words*. The Flesch Index also counts syllables. A high syllable count is a negative in figuring readability, and short words have a positive effect on index figures. Short words not only are easier to read, but they are often stronger. Some single-syllable words are among the strongest in our language: *love, hate, death, life, free, save.*

Here's a passage in which substituting shorter words improves readability.

Original: In the final weeks of the Nov. 5 special elec-tion, the escalating tension underscores the competitive-ness of the race and its national implications.

Revised: As tension rises in the final weeks before the Nov. 5 election, the national importance of that tough race is obvious.

Editors should target not only long words, but unnec-essary words. Be a welfare reformer — make every word work. Cut deadwood. Here are just a few examples of ways to save words:

Original: The group began with three different plans . . .
Revised: The group began with three plans . . . .

Original: The goal for the future . . . .
Revised: The goal . . . .

Original: But before the hearings take place, city plan-ners must . . . .
Revised: But before the hearings, city planners must . . . .

Original: Located at 2455 Ascension Blvd., the office is

expected to serve . . . .
Revised: The office at 2455 Ascension Blvd. is expected
to serve . . . .

Original: The museum's haunted house is located in the
basement and takes up 4,000 square feet of space . . . .
Revised: The museum's haunted house takes up 4,000
square feet in the basement . . . .

Original: The officer took his baton and hit Mr. Carroway
a couple of times.
Revised: The officer hit Mr. Carroway twice with his
baton.

Original: He managed to determine the project's deadline.
Revised: He determined the project's deadline.

Original: The president has made a request that employees give their support to community arts.
Revised: The president asked employees to support community arts.

Original: The equipment eventually will serve to make
reductions in maintenance cost over time.
Revised: The equipment eventually will reduce maintenance costs.

What you've read in this chapter boils down to this —
keep it simple. Simple does not mean writing down to
readers. It's writing to readers. If you wouldn't say it, don't
write it. Would you say the following?

The Senate Thursday broke a decade-long
impasse over telecommunications reform and
approved a sweeping measure that lawmakers

said will spur competition and affect every
American who watches television, accesses a
computer on-line service or talks on the telephone.

No. You'd probably say this:

The Senate ended a 10-year impasse Thursday
by approving telecommunication reforms that sen-
ators said would increase competition and affect
nearly every American.

You noticed, of course, that the first sentence was
packed with journalese, which was cut in the revision —
Thursday broke, *decade-long impasse*, *sweeping measure*,
spur competition. Also note in the revision the time location — after, not before, the verb. How many times have
you said "I Thursday wrote" or "I Thursday voted"?
Never, most likely. It's not natural.

Exercises

• Find in a publication a lengthy sentence that works
— 50 words or more. Explain why it works. If you had to
tighten that sentence, could you do it without harming it?
If your answer is yes, rewrite it.

• Get five examples of passive voice in published articles. Rewrite them in the active voice and explain how the
change helped or harmed the sentences.

• Look again at the Rockne plane crash passages in
Chapter 4. Read Revision No. 2. Edit that version to make
it tighter and stronger. Keep the same format, but take out
deadwood and irrelevant information. Explain your editing.

Chapter 6

How can I tell you?
Quotations should be simple and direct

I quote others in order the better to express my own self.
— Montaigne

Quotations add life, authority, and veracity to a story
— if they are clear and concise. People being interviewed
do not always provide sparkling sentences. They often
misuse words, ramble, and take shortcuts. Editors should
not be slaves to the quoted word. Paraphrase when necessary. Cut when necessary. Always keep the reader in
mind.

If part of a quote is strong, use that part and paraphrase the rest. If you find only weak quotes in a story,
don't be shy about paraphrasing and cutting. A story with
no direct quotes is not like an emperor with no clothes.
Readers won't laugh; they probably won't even notice if
the story is well crafted. Readers would rather understand
all the story than struggle with fuzzy quotations.

"Well, that's exactly what he said" is no excuse. The
words may very well be the exact words of the speaker, but

that's no reason to inflict them on the reader. Subject the quoted word to the same rigorous editing that you use in the rest of the story. Once when I took a particularly poor quotation to a desk editor for clarification, the editor's response was yes, it's bad, but it's the only quote in the story. That's no justification for including material that is bound to damage the story.

In the following example, the speaker wanders and repeats. Every sentence in the quote needs help, so just forget the quotation and paraphrase. In some cases, a strong sentence can be saved and the rest paraphrased. That is not the case here.

Original: "I will be able to vote for it, but I'm not real excited we're cutting the building fund and cash reserve," Mrs. Lamberty said. "I fear that in a year or two, we'll be putting ourselves in some problems. I think we'll end up in some trouble over it."

Revised: She will vote for the budget, Mrs. Lamberty said, but she fears that cutting the building fund and cash reserve will cause problems in a year or two.

Be wary of the quotation fragment. When writers have awkward quotes, they are often tempted to pick a word or a few to enclose in quotation marks and paraphrase the rest. Why bother? Unless it is necessary to let the reader know that the words enclosed in quotes are the *exact* words of the speaker, just paraphrase the whole sentence.

Sometimes, fragment quotes can be mistaken for irony — *After the 60-0 loss, the coach said his team played a 'wonderful' game.* In that sentence, quotation marks are necessary to show irony, that the coach did not actually believe the game was wonderful. So, when you use fragment quotes, you risk misleading the reader, and the unnecessary punctuation can hamper readability. The best way to deal with awkward quotations is to paraphrase them or drop them. Use fragments rarely.

Exercises

• In publications, find five ineffective quotations that either should be paraphrased or cut. Explain why, and paraphrase the quotations that can be.

• Find five published quotations that work, and explain why they work.

Chapter 7

Oops!
Red flags for some common grammar errors

*Caress every sentence gently and soon it will turn into
a smiling expression.*
— Anatole France

Grammar, spelling, punctuation, and usage are important elements of clear and effective writing. We have been discussing guidelines for editing — flexible standards to make writing more readable. For the most part, grammar, spelling, punctuation, and usage are governed by rules. Over time, those rules may change, especially those for usage. That's why dictionaries change and sometimes differ. Language is a living thing, and it changes just as society and our environment change.

The rules of language are meant to assure that all who use the language understand each other. Further, writers whose work is flawed by grammar and other mechanical errors risk losing credibility and the reader's respect. As language grows and changes, there is often disagreement between those who oppose change and the advocates of change. For example, the need of a comma before *and* in a series has its pros and cons. Journalists tend to drop it; others keep it. Interpretation of the sequence of tense rule, particularly in sentences where the main verb is *said*, can sometimes bring copy editors to strong words. Most journalists ignore the tense sequence rule, and perhaps in time it will change.

Serial comma use and variations on the sequence of tenses with *said* rarely affect clear communication. However, the fact that sometimes relaxation of those rules may affect communication is reason enough to mind them. A car's engine will not function properly with a wrong or defective part, and a sentence will not communicate clearly if its parts are not in harmony.

Serial commas

To illustrate the problem, here are situations involving the serial comma.

Budget cuts will affect the departments dealing with transportation, law enforcement, waste disposal and health and human services.

Dropping the serial comma after *disposal* creates ambiguity. Readers do not know whether health and human services is a unit or two departments. Most will not argue about the use of the serial comma before the penultimate *and* in that sentence. In this version, however, use of the serial comma could be argued:

Budget cuts will affect the departments dealing with health and human services, law enforcement, waste disposal and transportation.

Defenders of the serial comma ask "why drop it?" It's the rule, and it does no harm. Opponents say it's not needed, so why bother. Just more clutter. But here's another example defenders might offer:

> City Council budget actions included cutting the transportation funding, minor adjustments to resolutions, debate on trash collection fees and increasing the law enforcement funding.

In that last version, readers do not know whether the budget actions included increasing the law enforcement funding or the debate included law enforcement funding.

A comma is needed after *fees* to make it clear that the increase was among the council's actions.

Tense

The following sentence is ambiguous because the tense is out of sequence:

> Mayor Tanya Hyde said she supports the severe budget cuts proposed at a public hearing last week.

Because the main verb, *said*, is past tense, the verb that follows, *supports*, must also be past, *supported*. An exception is when the second verb expresses a general truth. For example: The teacher said New Hampshire is (not *was*) north of Massachusetts. New Hampshire is north of Massachusetts and will remain there, barring some drastic shift in Earth's plates. That's a general truth.

Mayor Hyde's support is not a general truth. It's a position that could change. We can say Mayor Hyde *says* she supports . . ., implying by the present tense *says* that she continues her support. But when we report she *said* (in the past), the verb that follows *said* must agree with it.

Now, let's discuss some of the most common grammar errors. This is not a complete list of common errors; it discusses only those that writers most frequently make.

Pronoun errors

The following sentences contain pronoun errors.

1. Alexandra is younger than *her*.

2. The judges gave medals to Gorsky, Randol, and *myself*.

3. This conflict is between you and *I*.

4. Players from both teams planned to cheer *whomever* succeeded.

The form of pronoun needed depends upon whether it is a subject or object in the sentence. If it's a subject, it acts: *I, he, she, they, we, who,* for example. And if it's an object, it receives the action: *me, him, her, them, us, whom,* for example. *Self* pronouns are neither subjects nor objects but reflexives (*I* cursed *myself*) or intensifiers (*they* all think it's right, but *I myself* don't think so).

1. "Alexandra is younger than *her*" actually says "Alexandra is younger than she is." Therefore, you need the subject *she* for the verb *is* — even though the verb is understood rather than spoken. (You would not say "younger than *her* is.")
Corrected: Alexandra is younger than *she*.

2. If you remove *Gorsky* and *Randol* from "The judges gave medals to Gorsky, Randol, and *myself*," you'll see right away that you need an object for the preposition *to*. Not "gave medals to *myself*," but "gave medals to *me*."
Corrected: The judges gave medals to Gorsky, Randol, and *me*.

3. You often can find out if you need a subjective or objective pronoun by substituting some other pronoun. Take the sentence, "This conflict is between *you* and *I*." Remove *you and I* and use other pronouns: "The conflict is between *we*, between *they*, between *us*, between *them*." Again, you see clearly that the subject *we* or *they* is wrong and the object *us* or *them* is right. So we'd need the objective pronoun in all cases.

Corrected: This conflict is between you and *me*.

4. The substitution game also is useful in settling *who/whom* arguments. (*Who* is the subject, *whom* the object.) Nobody has a problem with "Who called?" But change that to "Who *did you say* called," and many want to make it *whom*. Yet it's the same sort of sentence: "You did say *she*, *he*, *they* called?" Again, the pronouns *she*, *he*, or *they* show that you need the subject *who*, not the object *whom* — you would not say "You did say *him* called?

"Players from both teams planned to cheer *whomever* succeeded." The correct choice is *whoever*. Such sentences are confusing because you want an object for *cheer*, yet you also need a subject for *succeeded*. In these cases, the subjective pronoun wins. And the whole clause *whoever succeeded* acts as the object for *cheer*.

Corrected: Players from both teams planned to cheer *whoever* succeeded.

Agreement errors

1. Alexandra is one of those officials who *wants* to argue every point.

2. At the budget hearing, the mayor asked the *audience* if *they* were beginning to feel like *a vote* rather than *a citizen*.

3. The Royal Rug *Company* will close *their* store on Main Street.

4. *Everyone* who believes *they* can manage city finances should talk to the mayor.

5. Haricot says he agrees with *what seems* to be committee attempts to reduce spending.

1. "Alexandra is one of those officials who *wants* to argue every point." *Wants* is wrong here; the writer is making the verb agree with *one*, but the pronoun *who* (which in turn refers to the plural *officials*) dictates the verb: *officials who want*. This sentence says: *Among the officials who want to argue every point, she is one.*

Corrected: Alexandra is one of those officials who *want* to argue every point.

2. "At the budget hearing, the mayor asked the *audience* if *they* were beginning to feel like *a vote* rather than *a citizen*." *Audience* is an "it"; the word is a collective noun and is singular, and it shouldn't be followed by the plural *they*, which in turn doesn't agree with *a vote* or *a citizen*.

Corrected: At the budget hearing, the mayor asked *audience members* if *they* were beginning to feel like *votes* rather than *citizens*.

If you changed *audience members* to *audience*, it would agree with *a vote* or *a citizen*, but not with *they*. Then you'd have a troubling gender problem. Should you treat the masculine pronoun as neutral and use *he* instead of *they*? Or should you use *he or she*? You should do neither; both are awkward and create problems of their own. Best to make the antecedent plural — *audience members.* Another example: "Any *customer* wishing to exchange *his* (or *his or her*) gift must do so before Monday" should read: "Any *customers* wishing to change *their. . . .*"

3. Collective nouns (for example: *class*, *group*, *family*, *committee*, *team*, *company*) are usually singular in American English. The Royal Rug Company is an it: *its*

store. (But never *it's*, which is not possessive and means *it is*.) *Anyone*, *everyone*, *no one*, *anybody*, *everybody*, *nobody*, and *each* also are singular.

Corrected: The Royal Rug *Company* will close *its* store on Main Street.

4. "*Everyone* who believes *they* can manage city finances should talk to the mayor" should be recast to fix the *everyone/they* agreement problem.

Corrected: *All* who believe *they* can manage city finances should talk to the mayor.

5. "Haricot says he agrees with *what seems* to be committee attempts to reduce spending." *What* can be either singular or plural, depending upon the sentence. Here, the *what* refers to *attempts*, so the verb should be *seem*, not *seems*. If the *what* referred to one *attempt*, however, *seems* would be correct.

Corrected: Haricot says he agrees with *what seem* to be committee attempts to reduce spending.

Subjunctive errors

1. If it *was* up to Alexandra, no department would have to cut spending.

2. Gorky wishes he *was* a gold medal winner.

3. She acts as if she *was* mayor for life.

Use *were* with sentences that express wish or with "if" sentences that are contrary to fact: If I *were* queen; I wish you *were* going; Sam says that if he *were* president. . . . (I'm not queen; you aren't going; Sam isn't president.)

1. "If it *was* up to Alexandra, no department would have to cut spending" should be "If it *were* up to Alexandra, no

department would have to cut spending." This "if" sentence is contrary to fact (it's *not* up to Alexandra).

2. *Were* is the correct choice, as well, in "Gorky wishes he *were* a gold medal winner." Gorky is *not* a gold medal winner.

3. "She acts as if she *were* mayor for life." She is *not* mayor for life.

Note: Some writers overcorrect and use *were* with most if not all *if* sentences:

• I wondered if he *were* a winner. Wrong — the sentence is past tense, not subjunctive. Should be *was*.

• If I *were* rude, I'm sorry. Also wrong. It's not necessarily contrary to fact: I might have been rude. Should be *was*.

• If it *were* July, I might have been in Australia. Should be *was*; the month is not necessarily contrary to fact.

Likely errors

Likely is not a synonym for *probably*. *Likely* is usually an adjective, parallel to the adjective *probable*, rather than to the adverb *probably*. Not all words ending with *ly* are adverbs.

Likely behaves like an adjective when a *be* verb precedes it: The situation is likely to worsen. Not: The situation likely will worsen.

Faulty: They *likely* will win.

Better: They are *likely* to win.

Or: They *probably* will win.

Faulty: Bush *likely* will follow his father's policy regarding Iraq.

Better: Bush is *likely* to follow his father's policy regarding Iraq.

Or: Bush *probably* will follow his father's policy regarding Iraq.

(Exception: When the superlatives *very* or *most* precedes the word *likely*, *likely* behaves like an adverb: *They most likely will win.*)

That and *which* errors

Relative pronouns *that* and *which* have separate functions in introducing adjective clauses. *That* is restrictive, and *which* is nonrestrictive. A *that* clause is essential to the meaning of the sentence and is not set off by commas. A *which* clause is not essential to the meaning. It is parenthetical, and it is set off by commas.

• The librarian said she would destroy all the books *that* were damaged in the flood.
• The librarian said she would destroy all the books, *which* were damaged in the flood.

In the first sentence, the *that* clause tells us that only those books that were damaged in the flood will be destroyed. If the *that* clause is dropped, the meaning of the sentence changes. Therefore, it is restrictive.

In the second sentence, the *which* clause tells us that all the books were damaged in the flood. If we drop the *which* clause, the sentence meaning is not changed. Therefore, it is nonrestrictive.

Exercises

• Which common errors in this chapter give you the most trouble? Explain why and write a plan to rid your writing of those errors.

• Find in any publication five examples of the any of the grammar errors cited in this chapter. Fix them.

• Correct the errors in the following sentences. Answers are on page 158.

1. The new city manager likely will seek an increase in the budget.

2. The newest member of the council is younger than me.

3. Addison's committee approved a change in their meeting time.

4. Everyone who voted to change the meeting place said they did so because of the poor lighting in the old room.

5. The mayor said he is not a member of the group opposed to raising taxes.

6. If he was a council member, Canston said, he would vote for the project.

7. No one voted for the street project which was supported by the citizen committee.

8. Mayor Smith praised committee members Walker, Adderly, and myself.

9. What occurs in this meeting is between you and I.

10. The manager accepted the petitions from whomever showed up at the meeting.

Chapter 8

Show me:
Description readers can see

My task is to make you hear,
to make you feel — it is,
before all, to make you see.
— Joseph Conrad

This chapter is background for editing. Editors generally cannot change descriptive writing because they have not witnessed the event being described. But editors can and should work with writers to give readers a better word picture. When descriptive passages are weak or vague, you can talk writers through the description by asking what they saw, heard, smelled, felt, etc.

Writing good description is difficult, and editors with a feel for description can help both novice and gifted writers improve. This chapter has examples and suggestions for developing a sense of description.

Writers can create pictures with words — describing people, places, and things in such a way that the reader shares the writer's experience. Description should rely more on showing words than telling words. Telling words force the reader to interpret the scene that the writer is trying to describe. They are abstract. Showing words, whether active or static, bring the reader to the scene. They are concrete. Telling words are short cuts; they are conclusions. The writer who uses only telling words skips the details of the fireworks display and writes conclusively that it is beautiful, leaving the reader to imagine how a beautiful fireworks display looks, smells, feels, and sounds.

Good description needs carefully chosen strong, visual words, and when possible, action words. As Mark Twain observed, "The difference between the right word and the nearly right word is the same as the difference between lightning and the lightning bug."

When editing descriptive passages, try to imagine the scene that the writer is describing. Suggest to the author some words and concepts to which readers can relate. Sometimes writers can use a common experience to make a complex picture clear. See what Isaac Asimov does in this sentence from an article on electrical energy:

> When electricity flows through a wire or any
> other conducting material, it has to force its way
> through a crowd of atoms and molecules.

Readers can relate to that situation — forcing one's way through a crowd. Asimov is using analogy and action showing.

In this passage, novelist John LeCarre´ uses both action and static showing: "The engine was still running, shaking the car with inner pains. A wiper juddered uselessly over the grimy windshield." LeCarre´ carefully amplifies strong action words with vivid modifiers: *shaking . . . with inner pains* and *juddered uselessly over the grimy windshield*. Engines certainly do not have pain, but the metaphor lets us feel the shaking. *Juddered* is onomatopoeic, showing sound and movement. Modifiers are static words — *uselessly* and *grimy* — and they complete the picture.

Action showing has movement: *The quarterback lowered his arms slowly and trotted toward the bench.* Static showing has no movement, but helps readers see: *His face was the color of chalk dust, a sharp contrast with his flaming red hair.*

Note the difference in these two reports of the same event:

• *Kristi Yamaguchi wanted to keep the night romantic. But somebody put on the Blue Danube Waltz, and the crowd went wild.*

• *As Kristi Yamaguchi floated airily around the arena stenciling figures in the Olympic ice, all around the world, little girls were watching.*

Which one relies on telling and which on showing? Which gives you a clearer picture of Yamaguchi's Olympic appearance? Certainly, the second passage is visual — *floated airily, stenciling figures.* You can close your eyes and see Yamaguchi on the ice. Close your eyes after reading the first passage, and you see nothing. You hear music and applause. Yamaguchi is not in the picture.

Writing good description is not formulaic. It requires careful observation, much thought, keen imagination, and the right words. And in some cases, the right numbers. Numbers are not necessarily dull. This *New York Times* passage from a story on a party at the Museum of Modern Art employs numbers to paint a picture of the size of the party. *The Museum served 80 cases of champagne — which amounted to 960 bottles, or 7,680 three-ounce drinks to five thousand guests.* The numbers, in several dimensions, emphasize the magnitude of the party.

Specific figures can help the reader see. But sometimes analogy works as well. Truman Capote describes the size of Leavenworth's correctional facilities: *If all the inmates in these institutions were let free, they would populate a small city.* Capote isn't citing statistical evidence. He's drawing a word picture.

Here are a few more word pictures, employing various descriptive devices:

These are, to be exact, spotted salamanders. Black, six inches long and spotted with bright yellow polka dots, they resemble baby alligators in overtight clown suits.

—David Stipp
The Wall Street Journal

It's a quiet site. You can hear the gentle sizzling of high-tension wires from the electrical substation serving the construction works. Hundreds of pre-cast concrete tunnel segments lie baking in the sun — Snack Chips of the Gods.

—William Grimes
The New York Times Magazine

The evening air was pale and chilly and after every charge and thud of the footballers the greasy orb flew like a heavy bird through the grey light.

—James Joyce
A Portrait of the Artist As a Young Man

Birds do it. Bees do it. And sometime next spring Joe Cinquanta plans to do it too — over the Grand Canyon. Flap his wings and fly, that is.

—Bill Richards
The Wall Street Journal

I went back to my little bus, washed the strawberry field off me, ate a sandwich of something, opened a can of beer I'd bought from the last wet county, and looked through the windshield. Cars and trucks drove by. Some were noisy. Some were not. Sometimes a beer can flew out a car window. Once somebody shouted from a pickup. A dog peed on a mailbox.

—William Least Heat-Moon
Blue Highways

Hirschfeld's old face, with its sparkly eyes and hair that seems to grow in the wrong direction round his head, is that of a mischievous self-made man who is clearly in love with his creator.

—Simon Sebag Montefior
The New Republic

Good descriptive writing also demands discipline and focus. The search for the right words should end with a few. Don't clutter the picture with unnecessary detail, especially in the lead. Identify your subject and crop your picture tightly. Don't overwrite as this writer did:

An orange sherbet sunset melts into the Dallas skyline as the 9-to-5 inhabitants of the inner city slowly edge toward their destinations.

There's a pileup on Loop 12 and a disabled truck off R.L. Thornton at Fair Park. Headlights stretch like a strand of white twinkle lights across Central Expressway as the scene fades to black.

Nestled in the middle of the workday madness of ringing telephones and crunching bumpers sits a dimly lit pocket of comfort. The only thing with a ring is cigarette smoke curling into the Busch beer lamp over the pool table and fender bending is replaced by the crack of the cue ball sending the seven into the corner pocket.

This is Palms Danceland, open for daytime dancing and drinking 9 a.m. to 6 p.m. for most of the last 30 years.

It is a haven . . . .

Or this writer:

The freshly watered, painter's palette mix of *Viola wittrockinia* (pansies) planted near the waterfall at the Fort Worth Botanic Gardens glistened and shimmered in yesterday's hot, late-afternoon sun. The smell of earth and water and plant life wafted on a kite-dreamer's breeze.

A few feet away, the *Miscanthus sinesis 'zebrinas'* (zebra grass) stood pale and strawlike in the unseasonable heat; temperatures reached 86 degrees at Dallas/Fort Worth Airport, 21 degrees higher than the date's normal high.

So never mind the notice printed at the Botanic Gardens' main entrance saying that winter remains in effect, according to the seasonal hours that the peaceful urban Eden maintains.

Never mind that after two more days of luxurious warmth, forecasters say, the mercury will spiral downward, the skies will cloud, the rains will fall again and a freeze may well settle in by Saturday.

Never mind what National Weather Service climatologist Donna Crider said yesterday: 'There's some cold air that's going to start coming in around Thursday. It's polar in origin, and it's going to take kind of a direct route down here.'

For 76-year-old . . . .

In those two examples, the writers are carried away on self-made clouds of words. They stirred their steaming pot of description and were blinded by the vapors. Think of the description pot as a soup kettle. Blends of compatible flavors make a tasty soup. Too many or the wrong flavors will spoil the broth.

In the first lead above, readers may well ask what do a sherbet sun, twinkling city lights, traffic accidents, telephone ringing, and smoke rings have to do with the Palms Danceland? Nothing compatible in that soup pot.

In the second lead, Latin names of plants, waterfalls, kites, and earth divert readers from the news — it's unseasonably hot, but that will change. The description is not only overwritten, it's unnecessary. It's a weather news story.

Exercises

• This set of exercises will test writers' and editors' ability to sense what is going on around them and then to translate those observations into word pictures. It will give editors an appreciation for description, and the difficulty writers encounter in producing it.

Imagine how you would describe yourself. Write down a few things and read them aloud. Is your word picture complete and accurate? Would you recognize yourself if you jumped from your screen into your office? It's difficult, isn't it? Any description is difficult. Try writing a few sentences on how to tie a shoe. You need pictures to help you. The shoe-tying exercise is a good lesson to remember — sometimes words alone just can't describe. Then you must use pictures. But in this exercise we're working without pictures — just words.

Just for practice, rewrite these sentences using showing words rather than telling words. Use your imagination.

1. The setting sun as seen from the Key West pier was beautiful and exotic.

2. Joe Glum's game-ending catch was dramatic and by far the most exciting moment of the series.

3. His expression was smug, and his hair unkempt.

Now, you do the observing. This exercise is designed to sharpen your descriptive-writing skills and to emphasize the benefits of revision.

Use your five senses — experiencing through sight, touch, smell, hearing, and taste your surroundings at a particular time. Then describe the experience of each sense in a sentence. Write just one sentence for each sense, keeping in mind that you are showing, not telling. Use actual observations — your lunch or dinner, driving to or from work or school, in a supermarket, etc. To help you, here are some examples of sentences others have written for this exercise:

For sight:

Moonlight and shadows danced a surreal tango upon my bedroom wall.

For smell:

The sweaty odor of garlic wafted out of the apartment next door.

For taste:

Soda bubbles exploded like sweet orange sparks in my mouth.

For hearing:

The tennis ball exploded off the racket and whistled through the autumn air.

For feeling:

The fresh-cut bristles of grass tickled my toes as I walked barefoot across the lawn.

The object is to use strong words that make your readers experience the same sensations that you experienced. Again, use showing words, not telling words. Rely more on verbs (action) than on adverbs and adjectives. First, you might try revising those five sentences above. They are good description, but they can be improved. That task will give you some idea of the toughness of the exercise.

After you have written your own five sentences, revise them. Make them stronger and more vivid.

To take some of the edge off this tough exercises, here are few laughs. These attempts at descriptive sentences were written by journalism students. Nothing has been changed. The spellings, structure, and words are from the original writing. As Dave Barry says, I'm not making this up.

In the peripherary of my eye, the stripes of the chair used for lounging is looming down at me as I eat on the ruff carpet.

The writer's second attempt: The stripes of the lounging chair loom down at me as I eat sitting on the ruf carpet.

Gusting vehemently, into the fan goes all the smoke and flavors of a cooking meal.

Second attempt: The fan humms, capturing the flavors of the meal I'm enjoying.

Your turn now. Write with your senses. Good words to you.

Chapter 9

Wired for readers:
Melding news service material

Words are, of course, the most powerful drug
used by mankind.
—Rudyard Kipling

Most newspapers rely on wire services for news outside their home area. Small papers may have only The Associated Press service, and a large paper may subscribe to several wire services. On occasion, editors may receive several versions of a major news story. They have a choice: use one or merge the best parts from each into one story.

Usually, there is not much difference in each story. Perhaps one will have a few details that were not in the others. The merging can be a simple task of transferring or rewriting a few sentences or paragraphs, or it can mean rewriting the entire story using material from several wire stories. In any case, the editor should be certain to let readers know that the story is a compilation of several stories. A credit line at the bottom is generally sufficient, saying which wire services contributed to the story. When a story is mainly from one service with only a few lines picked up from another, editors might retain the original wire service byline at the top and mention at the end of the story that other services contributed to the report.

Always keep your readers in mind. The editor's job is to take the best information from several stories to produce the most complete and concise story for readers. However, be careful when merging that you don't pick up interesting but unrelated bits of information. Keep the story's focus and keep it tight. One danger in merging is that an editor may collect several quotations that say the same thing in slightly different ways. Once is enough. You can report unanimous support for an issue by saying just that in a summary sentence — no need to quote several supporters.

In other words, don't overmerge. That's as bad for the reader as overwriting.

In most cases, a design editor will assign a length for your story. That helps to keep a merged story reined in. Subject wire copy to the same rigorous editing you apply to copy from your staff.

Technology has made merging stories much easier. You can "cut and paste" electronically with a few simple keystrokes. In the days before electronic editing, editors literally cut material from one story with scissors and pasted it into another story — a messy job. In the days before glue sticks, editors sometimes mistakenly dunked a paste brush in a coffee mug in the rush to meet a deadline — ruining a nice cup of coffee. Today, the chief coffee hazard is spilling it on the keyboard.

Here are some suggestions for merging wire stories:

■ As always, read everything before you begin merging and editing.

■ Decide your method:
• Use one story with no merging.
• Use one story and merge information from others.
• Do a major revision with large blocks from each story

and some rewriting.

• Do a complete rewrite.

• Do any combination of mergers that serves readers best.

■ On your second reading mark or make notes on segments of each story that you want to retain.

■ Make an outline. It will help you to decide how much merging is needed and where merged or rewritten material will go.

■ If you are using one story and picking up material from others, cut and paste the portions you want to add to the main story.

■ If you are creating a new story from pieces of each, create a new story document and cut and paste material to that new file.

■ Rewrite as needed to give the material focus and transition. You may have to rewrite the lead as well.

■ When you have your material assembled in one document, begin the editing process. Rearrange segments, revise and trim if necessary. Keep in mind the length restrictions given to you by the design editor.

■ Remember to credit the wire services that contributed to your composite story.

Here are three wire service obituaries on Great Britain's Queen Mother. Read them all first, then go through them, noting passages you want to use, move, or change. The steps above are general suggestions. How you use those suggestions depends a great deal on your electronic editing system. Adapt your merging to suit your system and your comfort. Your design editor probably will give you a story length in column inches. Because column widths vary, I'll use word count as a measure. Merge and edit this story to 750 words. That's about one column of type in the average newspaper. Again, think of the readers as you merge and edit.

Story No. 1

The Washington Post

Queen Elizabeth, the Queen Mother, Britain's most durable and probably most beloved personality, died Saturday at the Royal Lodge in Windsor. She was 101.

A Buckingham Palace spokesman said the Queen Mother "had become increasingly frail in recent weeks following her bad cough and chest infection over Christmas." Her condition deteriorated and doctors were called in, he said, and she "died peacefully in her sleep."

The spokesman said Queen Elizabeth II, the Queen Mother's daughter, was at her side when she died. Her other daughter, Princess Margaret, died less than two months ago at age 71.

The Queen Mother had been consort to King George VI from 1936 to 1952, and she was mother of the reigning Queen of the United Kingdom of Great Britain and Northern Ireland. She was the matriarch of the royal family and a much-beloved icon of nostalgia for the British people. She was a last symbol to many of the nation's glorious 20th-century history, when Britain ruled the waves and an empire and stood alone for civilization against Hitler's hordes.

In the 1930s, she was credited with restoring

stability, and respectability, to a monarchy in crisis after the abdication of Edward VIII. In the 1940s, she pried her husband from his shell of self-doubt and helped to steel the national spirit against the bombs and deprivations of World War II. She remade the House of Windsor to appear more like a "family."

In the 1990s, when some of her grandchildren could not meet the new expectations, her own formula — detached dignity, strict silence on all matters personal, a smile and a wave — was cited by contrast as the model for the way royals ought to behave.

She lived the grandest possible life in the grandest possible circumstances and never bared a fragment of her soul. But by betting at the races, shooting pool and knocking back a pint for photographers, she won immense affection from millions of Britons as the royal with the common touch: the "Queen Mum."

The high point of her later years came as she led the nation in commemoration of the 50th anniversary of V-E Day in the summer of 1995, appearing on the balcony of Buckingham Palace as she had exactly 50 years earlier, before tens of thousands of people, many of them veterans, many of them weeping as the tiny (5 feet 2 inches) figure came forward through the huge palace doors.

A single controversy pursued her: She was said to be responsible for the virtual banishment from England of the Duke and Duchess of Windsor, for adopting and enforcing what some considered an excessively unforgiving attitude toward the dethroned king. In the scheme of her life, however, any residual bitterness was relegated to the realm of scholars.

"It is difficult to imagine someone so universally acceptable who is not insipid," satirist Auberon Waugh said of her on her 65th birthday. "There is nothing rude to say about her."

She was born Lady Elizabeth Bowes-Lyon six months before the death of Queen Victoria. The daughter of an ancient Scottish family, she was born in London and educated in the style of the city's wealthy families, at the knees of governesses and at Madame d'Egville's dancing school.

Recollections of her childhood and adolescence come largely from latter-day admirers whose memories were doubtless colored by her position. They are nonetheless a part of the Queen Mother's aura. Wrote David Cecil of his encounter with the child Elizabeth: "I turned and looked and was aware of a small, charming, rosy face, around which twined and strayed rings and tendrils of silken hair, and a pair of dewy gray eyes. Her flower-like mouth parted in a grave, enchanting smile, and between the pearly teeth flowed out tones of drowsy melting sweetness that seemed to caress the words they uttered."

Gushed another: She was "the most astonishing child for knowing the right thing to say."

She and her family moved in a small, elite circle that inevitably included the royal family, among them Albert Frederick Arthur George, second son of King George V and Queen Mary.

Early recollections of Albert, nicknamed Bertie, are the exact opposite of those of Elizabeth. She was outgoing, well-spoken, radiant with good health and flirtatious. He was awkward, stammering, knock-kneed, shy, sickly and frightened of girls — a "nervous wreck," as one historian would write.

The two became more acquainted in their twenties. His formidable mother was informed by a confidante that "he is very much attracted to Lady Elizabeth Bowes-Lyon. He's always talking about her. She seems a charming girl, but I don't know her very well."

On one pretext or another, Mary arranged a visit to the Bowes-Lyon home in Scotland and found she approved. Elizabeth, however, did not. Albert proposed repeatedly, and repeatedly she put him off.

A 1923 newspaper "scoop" — reporting that she was soon to be engaged to Albert's brother, Edward, the Prince of Wales, heir to the throne — brought Mary's intervention once again in a manner still uncertain but nonetheless effective. Shortly thereafter, Elizabeth accepted Bertie's proposal and the engagement was announced.

Reporters scurried the next day to her family's London home, where foolishly, it would transpire, she spoke to them.

"You are not wearing your engagement ring," said a reporter. "No," she responded. "It is to be made of sapphires."

"What were the circumstances surrounding the duke's proposal?"

"Yes, it is true that he proposed in the garden at Welwyn on Sunday. But the story that he proposed or had to propose three times — well, it amused me, and it was news to me. . . . Thank you so much. I am sorry there is so little I can tell you."

The king and queen were outraged that she had said anything and reprimanded her. It was the first, and last, interview Elizabeth would give. She remained throughout her life nonetheless press-conscious, always stopping, if briefly, for the photographers from Fleet Street. "I need them just as much as they need me," she once said.

Bertie had lived for years in the shadow of his bon-vivant older brother and had no expectations of becoming king. With the death in 1936 of George V, the throne did indeed pass to brother David — now King Edward VIII — and Elizabeth and Albert soon confronted the greatest crisis faced by the British monarchy in the 20th century.

The new king had been having an affair with Wallis Warfield Simpson — a twice-divorced Baltimorean — and was determined to marry her. The prospect of a "Queen Wally" — as poet Edith Sitwell wrote — "divorced twice too often for a Queen," appalled the family and Prime Minister Stanley Baldwin. Confronted with the choice of being king or marrying the woman he loved, Edward chose the latter and was forced to abdicate. The Duke and Duchess of York — Bertie and Elizabeth — became king and queen.

"Well," said Elizabeth, who had quickly recovered from a bout with the flu, "we must make the best of it."

Making the best of it included buying back from the ex-king Balmoral Castle and Sandringham — two royal residences — on the condition that he leave England forever. Communications between the brothers ceased.

While Elizabeth's specific role remains shrouded, most historians of the court attribute the hostile treatment of Edward to her. Her motives — it has been speculated — included personal outrage, worry about the image of the monarchy, and concern for image of her husband, inspired by the knowledge that the Duke of Windsor, as he became, would dominate media attention by remaining in Britain.

Elizabeth set about repairing the public relations damage, creating what came to be called "the Windsor Formula" — a "magic dispensation," as one chronicler expressed it, that enabled the monarchy to survive and prosper. She had already begun work on her husband's image, persuading him to seek help for his stammer — treatment from a famed Australian speech therapist — so he could deliver royal messages on the radio.

She also tried to seem more like a regular mother presiding over a regular family, which then included today's queen, young "Lilibet." It was a difficult balance, as she saw it, reconciling a studied aloofness with appropriate gestures of populism, making the world's least ordinary of families seem, when necessary, ever so ordinary.

The war years, terrible as they were, proved the ideal stage for the new monarchy. During the Battle of Britain, the Luftwaffe bombed the country every night, wreaking havoc in London, particularly its working-class East End. Elizabeth visited wrecked cities, inspected factories, received refugees, and pretended (according to biographers) to be strictly observing rationing.

In September 1940, a Luftwaffe bomber flew into the heart of London and dropped six bombs on and around Buckingham Palace. The king and Elizabeth were uninjured, but afterward she uttered the words that would remain indelible in the national memory: "It makes me feel," she said, "I can look the East End in the face."

On Feb. 6, 1952, George VI, suffering from lung cancer and its complications, died. Elizabeth, the Queen Mother, was 51.

Advance obituaries for her have been written, filed away, and rewritten every year by every newspaper in Britain. She has outlived generations of obit writers. Published in place of their work, every five years for five decades on her Aug. 4 birthday, were special pullout sections, ever more reverential, ever more affectionate. These culminated in massive coverage of her 100th birthday in 2000.

A woman of remarkable stamina, she overcame various injuries and age. And with the help of the finest doctors and her staff, she went about her public duties with considerable vigor until nearly the end of her life.

Though she wore diamonds, owned thoroughbred horses, stayed with Franklin and Eleanor Roosevelt at Hyde Park, mingled with the likes of Noel Coward and J.P. Morgan, her careful attention to common folk in public appearances over the years made her seem, underneath it all, like someone to have tea with.

"Most of the population of Britain lives in the permanent illusion that they have met her personally," said a newspaper essay on the occasion of her 85th birthday.

(1,711 words)

Story No. 2

The Associated Press

LONDON — The Queen Mother Elizabeth, a symbol of courage and dignity during a tumultuous century of war, social upheaval and royal scandal, died Saturday in her sleep. She was 101 years old.

After years of frailty and ill health, the queen mother died "peacefully" at Royal Lodge, Windsor, outside London, Buckingham Palace said. Her death came seven weeks after the death of her younger daughter, Princess Margaret, at age 71.

Queen Elizabeth II was at her mother's side when she died. The queen mother had rarely been seen in recent months because of her failing health.

The queen mother "had become increasingly frail in recent weeks following her bad cough and chest infection over Christmas," said a palace spokesman, who was not named in keeping with tradition.

Prince Charles and his sons Princes William and Harry were "completely devastated" after being informed of the news on their skiing holiday in Switzerland, a royal spokesman said. Charles was very close to his grandmother, and was cutting short his vacation to return home on Sunday.

Britain's main television and radio channels interrupted regular programs with news of the death, which came during the four-day Easter holiday. National figures and ordinary people from all walks of life united in expressing admiration and grief for the queen mother.

The queen mother's body was expected to be moved to the Royal Chapel of All Saints in Windsor Great Park on Sunday morning. Funeral plans were expected to be announced Sunday with the ceremony scheduled to take place in Westminster Abbey in London.

Scores of mourners, some bearing flowers, gathered outside Windsor Castle after hearing the news. They stood at the castle gates, quietly talking among themselves. The bells of the nearby St. John the Baptist church tolled to mark the queen mother's death.

"She's like everybody's grandmother," said Sheila Livingstone, who left a bunch of flowers at the castle gates.

Prime Minister Tony Blair said the queen mother was a symbol of Britain's "decency and courage" and the whole nation would join with the royal family in mourning her death.

"During her long and extraordinary life, her grace, her sense of duty and her remarkable zest for life made her loved and admired by people of all ages and backgrounds, revered within our borders and beyond," he said.

Former Prime Minister Margaret Thatcher said the queen mother was "a wonderful queen and an extraordinary person."

"Her death is more than a source of grief to the royal family. It is an irreplaceable loss to the whole nation," she said.

A brief statement of condolence was issued from the Texas White House.

"The president and Mrs. Bush are deeply saddened by the death of the queen mother," said White House spokesman Gordon Johndroe, who was with the president at his Texas ranch.

The queen mother was as popular at the end of her life as she had been a half-century before.

She was best known to younger generations as the mother of Queen Elizabeth II and grandmother of Prince Charles. Remarkably sprightly despite her age, the queen mother was a fixture at royal occasions, delighting in mixing with the public and greeting people who flocked to meet her.

She helped restore confidence in the throne during unhappiness and scandals in the royal family during the last years of her life, as three of her four grandchildren divorced. The divorce of Prince Charles from Princess Diana and her death in 1997 in a car crash in Paris shook the British monarchy to its core amid widespread anger that the popular princess had been spurned by the royal family.

The unflagging respect for Elizabeth dated back to World War II, when alongside the public she endured German bombs raining down on London, visiting shattered homes.

The queen mother underwent extensive surgery in 1995 and 1998 for hip replacements, and in 2000, fell and broke her collarbone. Until a few months ago, she continued a regular schedule of public appearances that would have daunted a much younger person. When her health became very frail, she sometimes appeared in public on an electric cart that was christened the "queen mum mobile."

While admired for her dignity and sense of duty, the queen mother was also revered for enjoying life. She relished horse racing, social gatherings and was known to enjoy a drink.

The queen mother might have been expected to retire from public life when her husband, King George VI, died in 1952. But after their eldest daughter's succession to the throne, she took a new title, Queen Elizabeth The Queen Mother, and a full load of royal duties, which she carried into her 90s, delighting in meeting people from all walks of life.

The former Lady Elizabeth Bowes Lyon, daughter of a Scottish earl, was married in 1923 to Prince Albert, Duke of York, second son of King George V.

They had two daughters, Elizabeth and Margaret Rose, and lived quietly until 1936. The duke's elder brother succeeded to the throne that January as King Edward VIII, and by mid-December had abdicated to marry American divorcee Wallis Simpson.

The Duke of York took the throne as King

George VI, a reluctant monarch whom many believed unsuited to the job.

But the steadfastness and sympathy of the new king and his wife through the deprivation and danger of World War II cemented a bond with the nation that held the queen mother firmly in British affections for the next half-century.

(910 words)

Story No. 3

Chicago Tribune

The Queen Mum is dead. There is no other.

Britain's Queen Mother Elizabeth, the most beloved member of the royal family and one of the most popular monarchs of all time, died Saturday morning in her sleep at Windsor Castle.

She was 101 and had been suffering from a respiratory infection since Christmas.

"Her condition deteriorated this morning, and her doctors were called," said a palace spokesman.

She had recently expressed the wish to live to 114 so she could become the oldest living British person ever.

Her daughter, Queen Elizabeth II, was at her bedside when the end came. Her only other child, Princess Margaret, died last month at age 71.

Prince Charles said he was "completely devastated" by his grandmother's death and rushed back from a holiday at Klosters, Switzerland, with his two sons, Prince William and Prince Harry, to join his family at Windsor Castle.

Prince Andrew, his two daughters, Beatrice and Eugenie, and their mother, Sarah, Duchess of York, returned from Barbados, where they had been vacationing.

The public began laying flowers at Windsor Castle and Buckingham Palace immediately after the Queen Mother's death was reported.

A Scottish noblewoman more British than the largely German royal family she married into, the Queen Mother had been a fixture in her nation's life since 1936, when her husband was crowned King George VI and she became Queen Consort.

She helped restore public faith in the monarchy after the scandalous brief reign of her husband's brother, King Edward VIII.

As Queen during World War II, she set an example of courage and sacrifice by remaining in London during the "Blitz" when she had been urged to seek safety in Canada. She and her husband were a frequent presence among ordinary Britons who suffered during the bombing and she was active in many relief and war efforts.

Hitler called her "the most dangerous woman" in Britain because of her ability to boost British morale.

In later life, she continued to be active in charity and other good works as head or honorary head of more than 350 organizations. "During her long and extraordinary life, her sense of duty and remarkable zest for life made her loved and admired by people of all ages and backgrounds, revered within our borders and beyond," said British Prime Minister Tony Blair.

"We are all the poorer because this gracious lady has been taken from us," said the Archbishop of Canterbury. "Her unfailing dignity, devotion to duty and charm have been a precious part of our national life for as long as most of us can remember."

She was born Lady Elizabeth Angela Marguerite Bowes-Lyon on Aug. 4, 1900, during the reign of Queen Victoria. Her father was Scotland's Lord Glamis, later the 14th Earl of Strathmore. A 14th century ancestor was the Thane of Glamis, whose castle was previously home to King Macbeth of Shakespearean legend.

As a teen-ager, she helped tend to the wounded when her family castle was turned into a hospital during World War I — a conflict which took the life of her brother, Fergus.

Members of the royal family often visited Castle Glamis, and she was a bridesmaid at the wedding of King George V's daughter, Princess Mary.

A pretty debutante, she lived a largely social but unremarkable life until her engagement and marriage in Westminster Abbey in 1923 to Mary's brother, Prince Albert, Duke of York, who would become King George VI.

As Duchess of York, she was drawn with her husband into the West End social circle surrounding her brother-in-law, Edward, when he was Prince of Wales and, for nearly a year, king.

This included weekends at Edward's country castle retreat called "the Fort," where there were encounters with Edward's mistress, American divorcee Wallis Warfield Simpson, who according to some accounts treated the future queen contemptuously. Simpson, who was regarded by the British upper classes as a social climber, reportedly referred to Elizabeth as "mousy."

Simpson hoped to become queen herself, but objections from Prime Minister Stanley Baldwin, among others, compelled Edward to abdicate instead.

Many historians believe this act helped save the

monarchy — and British democracy — because Edward was a known German sympathizer and Britain shortly afterward went to war with Germany.

As the Duke and Duchess of Windsor, Edward and his wife spent the rest of their lives largely in exile from Britain.

George VI suffered from a stammer and felt he was in no way prepared to be king. His wife called the throne "an intolerable honor" but she was a pillar of strength for her husband in carrying out his duties. She helped him overcome his speech problems but could not persuade him to abandon the chain smoking that eventually killed him in 1952.

In 1948, on the occasion of their 25th wedding anniversary, he gave a speech citing his marriage as the inspiration for what he had been able to accomplish as king.

After the outbreak of war, Elizabeth was urged to take her two daughters to Canada to be out of harm's way, but she refused, remaining in Buckingham Palace with her husband. It was bombed in September 1940, at the height of the Blitz, but they escaped injury.

Their work during the war years undid the harm caused by Edward VIII and set a standard of rectitude and duty by which her daughter Elizabeth set her course when she became queen in 1952.

Only 25, she leaned heavily on the Queen Mother for advice and support — as would Lady Diana Spencer when she prepared for her marriage to Prince Charles in 1981. The Queen Mother was a conspicuous figure at Diana's funeral in 1997.

After leaving the throne, The Queen Mother established a residence at Clarence House in central London and a country retreat called Castle Mey in Scotland.

She continued her public duties as indefatigably as when she had been queen, serving as commandant in chief of the Army and Air Force Women's Services and Women in the Royal Navy, commandant in chief of the Royal Air Force Central Flying School, president of the British Red Cross and Chancellor of the University of London, among hundreds of other posts.

She was also colonel of the famous Black Watch regiment, whose pipers will be taking part in the mourning.

She was demonstrably taken aback in 1992 when protesters booed her unveiling of a London statue of Sir Arthur "Bomber" Harris, an RAF leader whose massive bombing attacks against German and other civilians came under criticism in the postwar era.

As the first Scotswoman ever to be queen, she was made Lady of the Thistle. An expert fisherman, she was also regarded as one of Britain's foremost horse racing figures. Author Dick Francis, her jockey before he turned to writing, called her the finest judge of horseflesh he had ever known.

She overcame a number of ailments and afflictions in her later years. Developing serious arthritis in her 90s, she had hip replacement surgery in 1995 and broke her other hip in a fall at the Sandringham horse stud farm in 1998. It was later replaced as well.

Though the expectedly elaborate funeral arrangements were not complete, the Queen Mother is expected to lie in state in Westminster Abbey's Westminster Hall in the exact spot her husband's casket was so honored in 1952.

She is to be buried alongside her husband in the George VI Memorial Chapel at Windsor. Her daughter Margaret's ashes, which have been kept at St. George's Chapel at Windsor since her Feb. 15 cremation, are to be interred with her in the same coffin.

The British Parliament is to be recalled into session so that its members may pay their respects.

© 2002, Chicago Tribune.

(1,288 words)

Now that you've read all three stories, let's decide on your merging method. There is no one way to merge, and the only consideration is giving the reader the best possible story from the several that you select for the merger. We'll look at these stories together, following this merger plan: Pick up portions from each of the three stories, organize them following the outline, and edit to about 750 words. A good plan is to copy the material that you may include in the final story and paste it to another document. When it is all assembled, you can cut out duplicated and weak passages, move information, and condense.

Let's go through the stories and mark passages that we want to keep. Wear two hats for this exercise — editor's and reader's. You are editing as you select passages for your composite story, and you are a reader as you assess interest, seek answers to questions, and put information in order. Here's the outline that we'll follow:

Focus:
Britain loses Queen Mother

Developments:
Death comes quietly
Elizabeth overcomes turmoil
Many pay tribute

Story No. 1

Story:

Queen Elizabeth, the Queen Mother, Britain's most durable and probably most beloved personality, died Saturday at the Royal Lodge in Windsor. She was 101.

Editor/Reader:

The lead is OK with a bit of adjustment. We'll probably keep it.

Story:

A Buckingham Palace spokesman said the Queen Mother "had become increasingly frail in recent weeks following her bad cough and chest infection over Christmas." Her condition deteriorated and doctors were called in, he said, and she "died peacefully in her sleep."

The spokesman said Queen Elizabeth II, the Queen Mother's daughter, was at her side when she died. Her other daughter, Princess Margaret, died less than two months ago at age 71.

Editor/Reader:

Good detail. We'll probably keep and tighten it.

Story:

The Queen Mother had been consort to King George VI from 1936 to 1952, and she was mother of the reigning Queen of the United Kingdom of Great Britain and Northern Ireland. She was the matriarch of the royal family and a much-beloved icon of nostalgia for the British people. She was a last symbol to many of the nation's glorious 20th-century history, when Britain ruled the waves and an empire and stood alone for civilization against Hitler's hordes.

In the 1930s, she was credited with restoring stability, and respectability, to a monarchy in crisis after the abdication of Edward VIII. In the 1940s, she pried her husband from his shell of self-doubt and helped to steel the national spirit against the bombs and deprivations of World War II. She remade the House of Windsor to appear more like a "family."

In the 1990s, when some of her grandchildren could not meet the new expectations, her own formula — detached dignity, strict silence on all matters personal, a smile and a wave — was cited by contrast as the model for the way royals ought to behave.

She lived the grandest possible life in the grandest possible circumstances and never bared a fragment of her soul. But by betting at the races, shooting pool and knocking back a pint for photographers, she won immense affection from millions of Britons as the royal with the common touch: the "Queen Mum."

The high point of her later years came as she led the nation in commemoration of the 50th anniversary of V-E Day in the summer of 1995, appearing on the balcony of Buckingham Palace as she had exactly 50 years earlier, before tens of thousands of people, many of them veterans, many of them weeping as the tiny (5 feet 2 inches) figure came forward through the huge palace doors.

A single controversy pursued her: She was said to be responsible for the virtual banishment from England of the Duke and Duchess of Windsor, for adopting and enforcing what some considered an excessively unforgiving attitude toward the dethroned king. In the scheme of her life, however, any residual bitterness was relegated to the realm of scholars.

"It is difficult to imagine someone so universally acceptable who is not insipid," satirist Auberon Waugh said of her on her 65th birthday. "There is nothing rude to say about her."

Editor/Reader:

Let's keep at least the first paragraph of this segment and perhaps condense some of the rest.

Story:

She was born Lady Elizabeth Bowes-Lyon six months before the death of Queen Victoria. The daughter of an ancient Scottish family, she was born in London and educated in the style of the city's wealthy families, at the knees of governesses and at Madame d'Egville's dancing school.

Editor/Reader:

Good beginning to her biography. Keep it.

Story:

Recollections of her childhood and adolescence come largely from latter-day admirers whose memories were doubtless colored by her position. They are nonetheless a part of the Queen Mother's aura. Wrote David Cecil of his encounter with the child Elizabeth: "I turned and looked and was aware of a small, charming, rosy face, around which twined and strayed rings and tendrils of silken hair, and a pair of dewy gray eyes. Her flower-like mouth parted in a grave, enchanting smile, and between the pearly teeth flowed out tones of drowsy melting sweetness that seemed to caress the words they uttered."

Gushed another: She was "the most astonishing child for knowing the right thing to say."

Editor/Reader:

Marginal. Probably won't keep it. Did you notice *gushed another?* Let's not pick up that.

Story:

She and her family moved in a small, elite circle that

inevitably included the royal family, among them Albert Frederick Arthur George, second son of King George V and Queen Mary.

Early recollections of Albert, nicknamed Bertie, are the exact opposite of those of Elizabeth. She was outgoing, well-spoken, radiant with good health and flirtatious. He was awkward, stammering, knock-kneed, shy, sickly and frightened of girls — a "nervous wreck," as one historian would write.

The two became more acquainted in their twenties. His formidable mother was informed by a confidante that "he is very much attracted to Lady Elizabeth Bowes-Lyon. He's always talking about her. She seems a charming girl, but I don't know her very well."

On one pretext or another, Mary arranged a visit to the Bowes-Lyon home in Scotland and found she approved. Elizabeth, however, did not. Albert proposed repeatedly, and repeatedly she put him off.

Editor/Reader:

This skips a part of her life. The story jumps from her birth to her marriage. Perhaps we can use some of this, but we need information that continues her biography.

Story:

A 1923 newspaper "scoop" — reporting that she was soon to be engaged to Albert's brother, Edward, the Prince of Wales, heir to the throne — brought Mary's intervention once again in a manner still uncertain but nonetheless effective. Shortly thereafter, Elizabeth accepted Bertie's proposal and the engagement was announced.

Reporters scurried the next day to her family's London home, where foolishly, it would transpire, she spoke to them.

"You are not wearing your engagement ring," said a reporter. "No," she responded. "It is to be made of sapphires."

"What were the circumstances surrounding the duke's proposal?"

"Yes, it is true that he proposed in the garden at Welwyn on Sunday. But the story that he proposed or had to propose three times — well, it amused me, and it was news to me. . . . Thank you so much. I am sorry there is so little I can tell you."

The king and queen were outraged that she had said anything and reprimanded her. It was the first, and last, interview Elizabeth would give. She remained throughout her life nonetheless press-conscious, always stopping, if briefly, for the photographers from Fleet Street. "I need them just as much as they need me," she once said.

Bertie had lived for years in the shadow of his bon-vivant older brother and had no expectations of becoming king. With the death in 1936 of George V, the throne did indeed pass to brother David — now King Edward VIII — and Elizabeth and Albert soon confronted the greatest crisis faced by the British monarchy in the 20th century.

The new king had been having an affair with Wallis Warfield Simpson — a twice-divorced Baltimorean — and was determined to marry her. The prospect of a "Queen Wally" — as poet Edith Sitwell wrote — "divorced twice too often for a Queen," appalled the family and Prime Minister Stanley Baldwin. Confronted with the choice of being king or marrying the woman he loved, Edward chose the latter and was forced to abdicate. The Duke and Duchess of York-Bertie and Elizabeth — became king and queen.

"Well," said Elizabeth, who had quickly recovered from a bout with the flu, "we must make the best of it."

Making the best of it included buying back from the ex-king Balmoral Castle and Sandringham — two royal residences — on the condition that he leave England for-ever. Communications between the brothers ceased.

While Elizabeth's specific role remains shrouded, most historians of the court attribute the hostile treatment of Edward to her. Her motives — it has been speculated — included personal outrage, worry about the image of the monarchy, and concern for image of her husband, inspired by the knowledge that the Duke of Windsor, as he became, would dominate media attention by remaining in Britain.

Elizabeth set about repairing the public relations damage, creating what came to be called "the Windsor Formula" — a "magic dispensation," as one chronicler expressed it, that enabled the monarchy to survive and prosper. She had already begun work on her husband's image, persuading him to seek help for his stammer — treatment from a famed Australian speech therapist — so he could deliver royal messages on the radio.

She also tried to seem more like a regular mother presiding over a regular family, which then included today's queen, young "Lilibet." It was a difficult balance, as she saw it, reconciling a studied aloofness with appropriate gestures of populism, making the world's least ordinary of families seem, when necessary, ever so ordinary.

The war years, terrible as they were, proved the ideal stage for the new monarchy. During the Battle of Britain, the Luftwaffe bombed the country every night, wreaking havoc in London, particularly its working-class East End. Elizabeth visited wrecked cities, inspected factories, received refugees, and pretended (according to biographers) to be strictly observing rationing.

In September 1940, a Luftwaffe bomber flew into the heart of London and dropped six bombs on and around Buckingham Palace. The king and Elizabeth were uninjured, but afterward she uttered the words that would remain indelible in the national memory: "It makes me feel," she said, "I can look the East End in the face."

Editor/Reader:

There's some good material in that passage, especially the last paragraph. Let's consider it and look for more biography of her youth.

Story:

On Feb. 6, 1952, George VI, suffering from lung cancer and its complications, died. Elizabeth, the Queen Mother, was 51.

Editor/Reader:

That's a terse paragraph. It's out of place here. But let's consider it.

Story:

Advance obituaries for her have been written, filed away, and rewritten every year by every newspaper in Britain. She has outlived generations of obit writers. Published in place of their work, every five years for five decades on her Aug. 4 birthday, were special pullout sections, ever more reverential, ever more affectionate. These culminated in massive coverage of her 100th birthday in 2000.

A woman of remarkable stamina, she overcame various injuries and age. And with the help of the finest doctors and her staff, she went about her public duties with considerable vigor until nearly the end of her life.

Though she wore diamonds, owned thoroughbred horses, stayed with Franklin and Eleanor Roosevelt at Hyde Park, mingled with the likes of Noel Coward and J.P. Morgan, her careful attention to common folk in public appearances over the years made her seem, underneath it all, like someone to have tea with.

"Most of the population of Britain lives in the permanent illusion that they have met her personally," said a newspaper essay on the occasion of her 85th birthday.

Editor/Reader:
That's optional. The last quotation is good. Keep it in mind.

Story No. 2

Story:
LONDON — The Queen Mother Elizabeth, a symbol of courage and dignity during a tumultuous century of war, social upheaval and royal scandal, died Saturday in her sleep. She was 101 years old.

Editor/Reader:
The lead is not bad, but the lead on Story No. 1 is better. This one sags in the middle — too much detail.

Story:
After years of frailty and ill health, the queen mother died "peacefully" at Royal Lodge, Windsor, outside London, Buckingham Palace said. Her death came seven weeks after the death of her younger daughter, Princess Margaret, at age 71.

Queen Elizabeth II was at her mother's side when she died. The queen mother had rarely been seen in recent months because of her failing health.

The queen mother "had become increasingly frail in recent weeks following her bad cough and chest infection over Christmas," said a palace spokesman, who was not named in keeping with tradition.

Editor/Reader:
Similar to the details in the first story. Keep it in mind but perhaps we won't pick it up.

Story:
Prince Charles and his sons Princes William and

Harry were "completely devastated" after being informed of the news on their skiing holiday in Switzerland, a royal spokesman said. Charles was very close to his grandmother, and was cutting short his vacation to return home on Sunday.

Britain's main television and radio channels interrupted regular programs with news of the death, which came during the four-day Easter holiday. National figures and ordinary people from all walks of life united in expressing admiration and grief for the queen mother.

The queen mother's body was expected to be moved to the Royal Chapel of All Saints in Windsor Great Park on Sunday morning. Funeral plans were expected to be announced Sunday with the ceremony scheduled to take place in Westminster Abbey in London.

Scores of mourners, some bearing flowers, gathered outside Windsor Castle after hearing the news. They stood at the castle gates, quietly talking among themselves. The bells of the nearby St. John the Baptist church tolled to mark the queen mother's death.

Editor/Reader:

Details we didn't get in the first story. It's out of place here, but let's save it.

Story:

"She's like everybody's grandmother," said Sheila Livingstone, who left a bunch of flowers at the castle gates.

Prime Minister Tony Blair said the queen mother was a symbol of Britain's "decency and courage" and the whole nation would join with the royal family in mourning her death.

"During her long and extraordinary life, her grace, her sense of duty and her remarkable zest for life made her loved and admired by people of all ages and backgrounds, revered within our borders and beyond," he said.

Former Prime Minister Margaret Thatcher said the queen mother was "a wonderful queen and an extraordinary person."

"Her death is more than a source of grief to the royal family. It is an irreplaceable loss to the whole nation," she said.

A brief statement of condolence was issued from the Texas White House.

"The president and Mrs. Bush are deeply saddened by the death of the queen mother," said White House spokesman Gordon Johndroe, who was with the president at his Texas ranch.

Editor/Reader:

Some good quotations. Let's keep them and see if we can fit some in the final story.

Story:

The queen mother was as popular at the end of her life as she had been a half-century before.

She was best known to younger generations as the mother of Queen Elizabeth II and grandmother of Prince Charles. Remarkably sprightly despite her age, the queen mother was a fixture at royal occasions, delighting in mixing with the public and greeting people who flocked to meet her.

She helped restore confidence in the throne during unhappiness and scandals in the royal family during the last years of her life, as three of her four grandchildren divorced. The divorce of Prince Charles from Princess Diana and her death in 1997 in a car crash in Paris shook the British monarchy to its core amid widespread anger that the popular princess had been spurned by the royal family.

The unflagging respect for Elizabeth dated back to

World War II, when alongside the public she endured German bombs raining down on London, visiting shattered homes.

The queen mother underwent extensive surgery in 1995 and 1998 for hip replacements, and in 2000, fell and broke her collarbone. Until a few months ago, she continued a regular schedule of public appearances that would have daunted a much younger person. When her health became very frail, she sometimes appeared in public on an electric cart that was christened the "queen mum mobile."

While admired for her dignity and sense of duty, the queen mother was also revered for enjoying life. She relished horse racing, social gatherings and was known to enjoy a drink.

The queen mother might have been expected to retire from public life when her husband, King George VI, died in 1952. But after their eldest daughter's succession to the throne, she took a new title, Queen Elizabeth The Queen Mother, and a full load of royal duties, which she carried into her 90s, delighting in meeting people from all walks of life.

The former Lady Elizabeth Bowes Lyon, daughter of a Scottish earl, was married in 1923 to Prince Albert, Duke of York, second son of King George V.

They had two daughters, Elizabeth and Margaret Rose, and lived quietly until 1936. The duke's elder brother succeeded to the throne that January as King Edward VIII, and by mid-December had abdicated to marry American divorcee Wallis Simpson.

The Duke of York took the throne as King George VI, a reluctant monarch whom many believed unsuited to the job.

But the steadfastness and sympathy of the new king and his wife through the deprivation and danger of World War II cemented a bond with the nation that held the queen mother firmly in British affections for the next half-century.

Editor/Reader:

Rambling biographical material. Perhaps we don't need anything from that segment.

Story No. 3

Story:

The Queen Mum is dead. There is no other.

Britain's Queen Mother Elizabeth, the most beloved member of the royal family and one of the most popular monarchs of all time, died Saturday morning in her sleep at Windsor Castle.

Editor/Reader:

No. The other leads are better.

Story:

She was 101 and had been suffering from a respiratory infection since Christmas.

"Her condition deteriorated this morning, and her doctors were called," said a palace spokesman.

She had recently expressed the wish to live to 114 so she could become the oldest living British person ever.

Her daughter, Queen Elizabeth II, was at her bedside when the end came. Her only other child, Princess Margaret, died last month at the age 71.

Editor/Reader:

Similar details except for the wish to live to 114. Perhaps we can pick that up.

Story:

Prince Charles said he was "completely devastated"

by his grandmother's death and rushed back from a holi-
day at Klosters, Switzerland, with his two sons, Prince
William and Prince Harry, to join his family at Windsor
Castle.

Prince Andrew, his two daughters, Beatrice and
Eugenie, and their mother, Sarah, Duchess of York,
returned from Barbados, where they had been vacationing.

The public began laying flowers at Windsor Castle
and Buckingham Palace immediately after the Queen
Mother's death was reported.

Editor/Reader:

The part about Andrew was not in the other stories.
Save it.

Story:

A Scottish noblewoman more British than the largely
German royal family she married into, the Queen Mother
had been a fixture in her nation's life since 1936, when
her husband was crowned King George VI and she
became Queen Consort.

Editor/Reader:

That statement about British-German background is
not in the others. Save it. Perhaps we can use it.

Story:

She helped restore public faith in the monarchy after
the scandalous brief reign of her husband's brother, King
Edward VIII.

As Queen during World War II, she set an example of
courage and sacrifice by remaining in London during the
"Blitz" when she had been urged to seek safety in Canada.
She and her husband were a frequent presence among
ordinary Britons who suffered during the bombing and she

was active in many relief and war efforts.

Hitler called her "the most dangerous woman" in Britain because of her ability to boost British morale.

Editor/Reader:

That biography is out of place, but the part about Hitler is good and perhaps we can use that in the final story.

Story:

In later life, she continued to be active in charity and other good works as head or honorary head of more than 350 organizations. "During her long and extraordinary life, her sense of duty and remarkable zest for life made her loved and admired by people of all ages and backgrounds, revered within our borders and beyond," said British Prime Minister Tony Blair.

"We are all the poorer because this gracious lady has been taken from us," said the Archbishop of Canterbury. "Her unfailing dignity, devotion to duty and charm have been a precious part of our national life for as long as most of us can remember."

Editor/Reader:

Not much there. The part about charity is a possibility for the final story.

Story:

She was born Lady Elizabeth Angela Marguerite Bowes-Lyon on Aug. 4, 1900, during the reign of Queen Victoria. Her father was Scotland's Lord Glamis, later the 14th Earl of Strathmore. A 14th century ancestor was the Thane of Glamis, whose castle was previously home to King Macbeth of Shakespearean legend.

As a teen-ager, she helped tend to the wounded when her family castle was turned into a hospital during World

War I — a conflict which took the life of her brother, Fergus.

Members of the royal family often visited Castle Glamis, and she was a bridesmaid at the wedding of King George V's daughter, Princess Mary.

A pretty debutante, she lived a largely social but unremarkable life until her engagement and marriage in Westminster Abbey in 1923 to Mary's brother, Prince Albert, Duke of York, who would become King George VI.

As Duchess of York, she was drawn with her husband into the West End social circle surrounding her brother-in-law, Edward, when he was Prince of Wales and, for nearly a year, king.

This included weekends at Edward's country castle retreat called "the Fort," where there were encounters with Edward's mistress, American divorcee Wallis Warfield Simpson, who according to some accounts treated the future queen contemptuously. Simpson, who was regarded by the British upper classes as a social climber, reportedly referred to Elizabeth as "mousy."

Simpson hoped to become queen herself, but objections from Prime Minister Stanley Baldwin, among others, compelled Edward to abdicate instead.

Many historians believe this act helped save the monarchy — and British democracy — because Edward was a known German sympathizer and Britain shortly afterward went to war with Germany.

As the Duke and Duchess of Windsor, Edward and his wife spent the rest of their lives largely in exile from Britain.

George VI suffered from a stammer and felt he was in no way prepared to be king. His wife called the throne "an intolerable honor" but she was a pillar of strength for her husband in carrying out his duties. She helped him overcome his speech problems but could not persuade him to abandon the chain smoking that eventually killed him in

1952.

In 1948, on the occasion of their 25th wedding anniversary, he gave a speech citing his marriage as the inspiration for what he had been able to accomplish as king.

After the outbreak of war, Elizabeth was urged to take her two daughters to Canada to be out of harm's way, but she refused, remaining in Buckingham Palace with her husband. It was bombed in September 1940, at the height of the Blitz, but they escaped injury.

Their work during the war years undid the harm caused by Edward VIII and set a standard of rectitude and duty by which her daughter Elizabeth set her course when she became queen in 1952.

Only 25, she leaned heavily on the Queen Mother for advice and support — as would Lady Diana Spencer when she prepared for her marriage to Prince Charles in 1981. The Queen Mother was a conspicuous figure at Diana's funeral in 1997.

After leaving the throne, The Queen Mother established a residence at Clarence House in central London and a country retreat called Castle Mey in Scotland.

She continued her public duties as indefatigably as when she had been queen, serving as commandant in chief of the Army and Air Force Women's Services and Women in the Royal Navy, commandant in chief of the Royal Air Force Central Flying School, president of the British Red Cross and Chancellor of the University of London, among hundreds of other posts.

She was also colonel of the famous Black Watch regiment, whose pipers will be taking part in the mourning.

She was demonstrably taken aback in 1992 when protesters booed her unveiling of a London statue of Sir Arthur "Bomber" Harris, an RAF leader whose massive bombing attacks against German and other civilians came under criticism in the postwar era.

As the first Scotswoman ever to be queen, she was made Lady of the Thistle. An expert fisherman, she was also regarded as one of Britain's foremost horse racing figures. Author Dick Francis, her jockey before he turned to writing, called her the finest judge of horseflesh he had ever known.

She overcame a number of ailments and afflictions in her later years. Developing serious arthritis in her 90s, she had hip replacement surgery in 1995 and broke her other hip in a fall at the Sandringham horse stud farm in 1998. It was later replaced as well.

Editor/Reader:

Good biographical details and in chronological order. Perhaps that segment can be condensed and used in the final.

Story:

Though the expectedly elaborate funeral arrangements were not complete, the Queen Mother is expected to lie in state in Westminster Abbey's Westminster Hall in the exact spot her husband's casket was so honored in 1952.

She is to be buried alongside her husband in the George VI Memorial Chapel at Windsor. Her daughter Margaret's ashes, which have been kept at St. George's Chapel at Windsor since her Feb. 15 cremation, are to be interred with her in the same coffin.

The British Parliament is to be recalled into session so that its members may pay their respects.

Editor/Reader:

Good conclusion. Save it.

After you have collected the information from the three stories, put them in order and edit the merged story.

The final version obviously will not have all the information you picked up from the three stories, but it should be complete, concise and in the area of 750 words.

When you have created a new document with all parts to be considered for your final version, move them into the order that you chose in your outline and run a word count. You'll then know how much you must trim to meet the design editor's specifications.

Then you're ready to edit. Treat the merged copy just as you handled stories in chapters above. Read as a reader, and edit professionally. Pay attention to organization in particular. It's easy to get material out of sequence when you are merging several stories.

Transition is also important. Pieces from several stories will need massaging to make them fit into the story flow. Sometimes simple transitional words such as *next*, *then*, *however*, *later*, *earlier*, etc., will be all that is needed. Other times, sentences may have to be rewritten to give them transition. Keep readers in mind.

The merged story is below. The origin of information is marked at the end of the merged passage with a story numeral in parentheses (1), (2), or (3). Some passages have been edited for transition or compression.

From Wire Services

Queen Mother Elizabeth, Britain's most durable and probably most beloved personality, died in her sleep Saturday at the Royal Lodge in Windsor. She was 101.

The Queen Mother had become increasingly frail in recent weeks following a chest infection at Christmas. Queen Elizabeth II, the Queen Mother's daughter, was at her side when she died. Her other daughter, Princess Margaret, died less than two months ago at age 71. (1)

She had been queen consort to King George VI

from 1936 to 1952, and she was mother of the reigning Queen of the United Kingdom of Great Britain and Northern Ireland. She was the matriarch of the royal family and a much-beloved icon of nostalgia for the British people. (1)

The Queen Mother was born Lady Elizabeth Angela Marguerite Bowes-Lyon on Aug. 4, 1900, during the reign of Queen Victoria. Her father was Scotland's Lord Glamis, later the 14th Earl of Strathmore.

As a teen-ager, she helped tend to the wounded when her family castle was turned into a hospital during World War I — a conflict that took the life of her brother, Fergus.

Members of the royal family often visited Castle Glamis, and she was a bridesmaid at the wedding of King George V's daughter, Princess Mary.

A pretty debutante, she lived a largely social but unremarkable life until her engagement and marriage in Westminster Abbey in 1923 to Mary's brother, Prince Albert, Duke of York, who would become King George VI. (3) Albert had lived for years in the shadow of his older brother and had no expectations of becoming king. With the death in 1936 of George V, the throne indeed passed to brother David — King Edward VIII — and Elizabeth and Albert soon confronted the greatest crisis faced by the British monarchy in the 20th century. (1)

The new king had been having an affair with Wallis Warfield Simpson, a twice-divorced American, and was determined to marry her. Confronted with the choice of being king or marrying the woman he loved, Edward chose the latter and was forced to abdicate. Albert became King George VI. (1)

After the outbreak of WWII, Elizabeth was urged to take her two daughters to Canada to be out of harm's way, but she refused, remaining in Buckingham Palace with her husband. It was bombed in September 1940 at the height of the Blitz, but they escaped injury.

The king's and queen's work during the war years undid the harm caused by Edward VIII and set a standard of rectitude and duty. Later, her daughter Elizabeth set her course by that standard when she became queen after her father died on Feb. 6, 1952, from lung cancer.

After leaving the throne, the Queen Mother continued her public duties as indefatigably as when she had been queen. She was active in charity and other good works as head or honorary head of more than 350 organizations.

She overcame a number of ailments and afflictions in her later years. Developing serious arthritis in her 90s, she had hip replacement surgery in 1995 and broke her other hip in a fall. It was later replaced as well. (3)

On Saturday, Britain's main television and radio channels interrupted regular programs to announce the Queen Mother's death. The public began laying flowers at Windsor Castle and Buckingham Palace immediately after the Queen Mother's death was reported.

"She's like everybody's grandmother," said Sheila Livingstone, who left flowers at the castle gates.

Elizabeth's grandson Prince Charles and his sons Princes William and Harry were to return Sunday from their skiing holiday in Switzerland, (2) and Prince Andrew, his two daughters, Beatrice and Eugenie, and their mother, Sarah, Duchess of

York, returned from Barbados, where they had been vacationing. (3)

Prime Minister Tony Blair, former Prime Minister Margaret Thatcher, President Bush, the Archbishop of Canterbury and other dignitaries, expressed condolences.

"Her death is more than a source of grief to the royal family. It is an irreplaceable loss to the whole nation," said Margaret Thatcher. (2)

Funeral arrangements were not complete, but the Queen Mother is expected to lie in state in Westminster Abbey's Westminster Hall in the exact spot her husband's casket was so honored in 1952.

She is to be buried alongside her husband in the George VI Memorial Chapel at Windsor. Her daughter Margaret's ashes, which have been kept at St. George's Chapel at Windsor since her Feb. 15 cremation, are to be interred with her in the same coffin.

The British Parliament is to be recalled into session so that its members may pay their respects. (3)

The Associated Press, Washington Post, and Chicago Tribune news services contributed to this report.

(751 words)

Exercises

• Go back to the original three stories in this chapter. Give yourself more space, perhaps 1,500 words, and do another merger. Write another lead, and perhaps try a different outline for your final story.

• Read three daily newspapers that report the same news event. It can be any subject — politics, tragedy, financial, sports, etc. Clip them. Merge information from the three stories into one. Explain how you did it and why.

Chapter 10

Toward better editing
Getting in shape and staying there

Everybody ought to do at least two things
each day that he hates to do, just for practice.
— William James

Editors may feel that they do enough editing at the office, and they don't need to practice outside work. That's fine if you don't want to improve. You need not be a boor about your profession, driving your family and friends away. But you do have to exercise your skills regularly, especially when you are away from the job and relaxed. In this chapter we'll discuss calisthenics for the mind.

If you are a student and want to be an editor or writer, do the same exercises but adapt them to your environment. Involve other journalism students and faculty. Read, write, and think. Athletes work out, pianists practice, so why shouldn't editors practice, too? You don't have to closet yourself in a room and edit piles of old stories. That's not productive. Think writing and editing. Think words and sentences.

Instead of browsing through last year's magazines as you wait in the doctor's office, look around you. Compose in your head sentences to describe what you see — the furniture, the people, the sounds, and perhaps the smells. If you create a phrase that you like, write it down. Think words and create in other places, too — on a plane, driving to work in your car, while dining, walking, exercising, etc. And if you're forced to read year-old magazines, look for passages that catch your interest or turn you off. Consider why, and note it.

Carry a small note pad with you. When you see something you might use in your work, write it down. It may be a sparkling sentence in a magazine, a catchy phrase on a billboard, something a friend said. Remember, you deal in words, and words that catch your attention — good or bad — will probably have the same effect on others, particularly your readers.

I've used an exercise that challenges the senses in writing classes and seminars. I pass a bag of popcorn around, ask each to take some, examine it, taste it, and write a description of it for someone who has never seen popcorn. Try it. Try it with potato chips, candy, ice cream, etc. Try describing how to tie a shoelace or necktie. You'll be surprised how difficult it is to rely on words to create a picture. We're so visual. We rely on diagrams, graphics, photos, television, movies, the Internet, etc. We're too often not challenged to explain or describe something in words. Keep such experiences in mind as you edit a writer's descriptive passages. Pass what you learn along to the writers with whom you work. Remember, you're all working for the readers.

Pay attention to what others in creative fields say and do. Artists, actors, directors, architects, home and fashion designers, and other writers and editors do the same things you do: they create works for people to enjoy. My wife and I watch and listen to broadcast interviews, and we have found it interesting that often what actors, musicians, and artists say about their craft also applies to writing. When we listen to these interviews, we're not just being entertained, we're practicing. We're learning.

Learn from your experiences, too. Don't be afraid to try something new. And encourage the writers you work with to experiment. It may be something as simple as adding a typographical device to enhance story transition, or it may be as complex as breaking up a long story into small anecdotes. You learn from experiences, even bad ones.

If your company does not conduct in-house workshops for writers and editors or sponsor staff attendance at outside seminars and workshops, lobby for it to begin doing so. Both writers and editors should attend the same in-house seminars. It's good to have the two groups together. They tackle the same problems, but from different angles.

However, you don't have to wait for your supervisor to set up a workshop. You can get a few writers and editors together informally and regularly to discuss writing and editing. The topics don't have to relate directly to work. You might want to read books on writing and discuss them. Or you might want to read interesting fiction and non-fiction and discuss techniques — narrative, description, dialogue, transitions, etc. You could meet for lunch or at weekend outings with the families. Critique each other's work. Invite local writers outside your company to join you. See a play or film together and discuss it. You can learn much from watching actors and directors at work. Good films and plays don't have dead spots. Good stories also should not have them.

Through all that discussion, observation and practice, keep a journal. It doesn't have to be a formal or expensive project. Get a notebook or loose-leaf binder from the school supply section of your supermarket. Write in it ideas, thoughts on writing and editing, paste clippings of stories and passages you like or dislike, comment on them, share your journal with colleagues.

Books and other reading

Anyone who works with words should read daily — books, magazines, newspapers, Internet reports, etc. Reading is part of practicing to be a better editor or writer.

Everyone has favorite authors, reading categories, etc. Read them and enjoy. But every so often, pick up a book that you might normally not read. It's good practice. Some in the media read only media-related books, magazines, and periodicals. The result is that they're all reading the same things and probably increasingly narrow. So read a mix of fiction and non-fiction. Try poetry. Read Shakespeare, Proust, the Bible. You'll be surprised by the experiences. Don't give up your regular reading, but make diversions into something new now and then. You don't have to read the whole Bible. Browse. One of the tightest leads ever is in the Bible: *In the beginning God created the heaven and the earth.*

In addition, you should have a good library of reference books on words, grammar, usage, etc. Here are a few of the reference books that I have found helpful:

■ A good dictionary and thesaurus or synonym finder.
There are many good ones. Select those that you are comfortable with.

■ *Hodges' Harbrace Handbook*, John C. Hodges, Robert Keith Miller, Winifred Bryan Horner, Suzanne Strobeck Webb; Heinle.
An easy-to-use and well-indexed grammar book.

■ *Rules for Writers: A Brief Handbook*, Diana T. Hacker; St. Martin's Press.
Another good grammar book that is easy to use and well-indexed.

■ *The Elements of Style*, William Strunk Jr and E.B. White; Macmillan Publishing Co.
  An old standard and a must for writers and editors.

■ *The Careful Writer*, Theodore M. Bernstein; The Free Press.
  A good usage reference by a former *New York Times* editor.

■ *Words on Words*, John B. Bremner; Columbia University Press.
  Another good usage book.

■ *Word Court* by Barbara Wallraff; Harcourt.
  A collection of comments on usage, grammar, etc. by a senior editor of *The Atlantic Monthly*.

■ *The New Fowler's Modern English Usage*, Third Edition, edited by R.W. Burchfield; Oxford.
  The latest revision of a classic book on usage. Detailed and an excellent resource.

■ *A Dictionary of Modern American Usage*, Bryan A. Garner, Oxford University Press.
  One of the most valuable and up-to-date writer's resources published in recent years.

■ *On Writing Well*, William Zinsser; Harper Collins.
  A good source of tips for writers. Helpful to anyone who writes.

■ *Writing for Story*, Jon Franklin; Penguin USA.
  Helpful book for organizing and writing features.

■ *The Art and Craft of Feature Writing*, William E. Blundell; Penguin USA.

Lots of material to help writers organize and write features.

■ *Follow the Story,* James B. Stewart; Simon & Schuster.
A good resource for developing and writing non-fiction.

■ *Line by Line,* Claire Kehrwald Cook; Houghton Mifflin Co.
A good guide to editing with clear explanations of grammar and usage.

■ *The Deluxe Transitive Vampire,* Karen Elizabeth Gordon; Random House.
An entertaining guide to grammar. Gordon makes learning proper English fun.

■ *The New Well-Tempered Sentence,* Karen Elizabeth Gordon; Houghton Mifflin.
An entertaining guide to punctuation. Gordon's examples will make you chuckle.

■ *Championship Writing: 50 Ways to Improve Your Writing,* Paula LaRocque; Marion Street Press, Inc.
A collection of Quill columns with many suggestions to improve writing and avoid common pitfalls.

■ *Bartlett's Familiar Quotations,* 17th Edition, John Bartlett; Little, Brown.
A great resource when you are looking for ideas for leads, ways to phrase something, or a famous quote to illustrate a point.

■ *On Writing,* Stephen King; Pocket Books.
An autobiographical book on writing with an abundance of advice for writers of any genre.

Exercises

• In your office or classroom, set up several reading clubs. Ask each group to appoint a chair person who will assign the group a book or magazine article each week. Members of each group will write and present a critique at the next meeting and the group will discuss the reading. Pay attention to reader interest. Your main question should be why was this interesting or not interesting reading. Note the author's style, voice, techniques, etc.

• Read "Mrs. Kelly's Monster" in Jon Franklin's book *Writing for Story*. Describe in detail Franklin's technique. As a reader, is there anything in Franklin's story that displeases you? Explain.

Answers to quiz on page 100

1. The new city manager **probably** will seek an increase in the budget.

2. The newest member of the council is younger than **I**.

3. Addison's committee approved a change in **its** meeting time.

4. **All** who voted to change the meeting place said they did so because of the poor lighting in the old room.

5. The mayor said he **was** not a member of the group opposed to raising taxes.

6. If he **were** a council member, Cranston said, he would vote for the project.

7. No one voted for the street **project,** which was supported by the citizen committee.

8. Mayor Smith praised committee members Walker, Adderly, and **me**.

9. What occurs in this meeting is between you and **me**.

10. The manager accepted the petitions from **whoever** showed up at the meeting.

Acknowledgments

A book grows on experience. It is impossible to remember everyone and everything that influenced this book on editing, but I'll try to recall some of the major inspirations and experiences. An easier task is thanking those whose contributions are obvious by their presence on the pages of this book. But thanks to all who influenced and helped in any way to produce this book.

Some of the anonymous examples in the book have been in my files for many years, and I've used them anonymously in lectures and workshops. Some may have been passed to me by a friend, a colleague, a student, or a workshop participant — their source unknown. But their value is not diminished by their anonymity. They are, after all, here for all of us to learn. In some cases, I have kept the source of a writing example anonymous in order not to embarrass editors and writers. Poor writing is not intentional, but it is ubiquitous. It's not the purpose of this book to chastise, but to help. Thanks to those anonymous helpers.

A great big thanks to my former colleagues at *The Milwaukee Journal*, where quality was always a necessary ingredient in writing and editing, and where I formed and enriched good writing and editing habits. They include Dick Leonard, Arville Schaleben, Paul Salsini, Tom Barber, Joe Shoquist, Howard Fibich, Ruth Wilson, Roger Miller, Dick Kienitz, Bill Nelson, Gary Rummler, Sandy Cota, Rod Van Every, Eddie Kaplan, Len Scheller, and

Charlie House. Their advice, patience, criticism, and kind words helped me through many deadlines.

Other colleagues in newsrooms, academe, and elsewhere whose support and comment have been invaluable include David McHam, Deanna Sands, Jim Flanery, Wally Sims, Bill Rivers, Tommy Thomason, Fred Stabley, Nick Vista, Ken West, Dion Henderson, Phil Seib, and Cecil Johnson.

Thanks to The Associated Press many times over, and especially for the tightly written short item on the errant casino ATM in Chapter 2. And to the Associated Press Managing Editors study committees whose reports on writing and editing provided tips, examples, and comments. Jon Franklin's *Writing for Story*, a favorite book that has helped me teach story organization, provided ideas and inspiration for Chapter 3. The disorganized "Survivor" story of Chapter 2, in which names have been changed, is from an anonymous source.

Former academe colleagues Tommy Thomason and Mark Witherspoon provided material for the cliché leads in Chapter 4. And items from several sources provided examples of good and bad Zimmerman leads in that same chapter. The items on the Nebraska patrolman and Rockne anniversary came from unknown sources in the Midwest; the mall traffic and Eldon George lead are from metro newspapers.

Some books have been particularly helpful to me and should be every writer's friends. Herman Melville's *Moby Dick* is the source of the excellent example in Chapter 5 — a long sentence that works. Rudolph Flesch (*The Art of Readable Writing*) and Robert Gunning (*The Technique of Clear Writing*), mentioned in Chapter 5, have helped me through their readability indexes to provide numerical evidence of overwriting for many lectures and face-to-face critiques. The school stories, and the teamster and drowning stories in Chapter 5 are from anonymous metro daily papers. The lengthy but great lead on Mayor Ed Koch is by the AP's Saul Pett. And thanks to Richard Lederer for his books and lectures, which provide constant support for using short words.

The quote in Chapter 6 on budget cutting is from a metro daily. For Chapter 7, which deals with troublesome words, thanks to the many students and writers whom I've helped wrestle with heavyweight grammar problems, and my wife, Paula, whose language diligence has helped keep my own grammar in line. Her comments and inspiration helped me over some of the tough bumps encountered in writing this book.

The chapter on descriptive writing owes thanks to many writers. Some are specifically mentioned in the chapter, but others contributed as well, if only through their inspiration. I'll mention a few favorites — Elizabeth George, Elmore Leonard, John McPhee, Garrison Keilor, Ruth Rendell, Stephen Ambrose, Bill Blundell, William Zinsser, and Stephen King. Also in that chapter, thanks to the students and workshop participants who provided material (some of it humorous) and suggestions for the exercises on writing for the senses. The weather and dance hall stories are from anonymous metro dailies.

A great big thanks to Nancy-Allison Stewart and the copy desk crew at *The Dallas Morning News* for collecting and passing along several examples of wire stories on the death of Queen Elizabeth. Each wire service took a slightly differing approach to the same information, providing an excellent resource to illustrate how an editor can use all to produce a story of the length and content to fit his or her publication's need.

And thanks to my publisher and editor, Ed Avis, for his patience and guidance.

Index

OTHER BOOKS FOR JOURNALISTS FROM MARION STREET PRESS, INC.

CHAMPIONSHIP WRITING
50 WAYS TO IMPROVE YOUR WRITING
BY PAULA LAROCQUE, $18.95

THE BOOK ON WRITING
THE ULTIMATE GUIDE TO WRITING WELL
BY PAULA LAROCQUE, $18.95

MATH TOOLS FOR JOURNALISTS
BY KATHLEEN WICKHAM, $16.95

PEN & SWORD
A JOURNALIST'S GUIDE TO COVERING THE MILITARY
BY ED OFFLEY, $24.95

UNDERSTANDING FINANCIAL STATEMENTS
A JOURNALIST'S GUIDE
BY JAY TAPARIA, $24.95

THE DICTIONARY OF CONCISE WRITING
10,000 ALTERNATIVES TO WORDY PHRASES
BY ROBERT HARTWELL FISKE, $19.95

THE DIMWIT'S DICTIONARY
5,000 OVERUSED WORDS AND PHRASES AND ALTERNATIVES TO THEM
BY ROBERT HARTWELL FISKE, $19.95

THE RENEGADE WRITER
A TOTALLY UNCONVENTIONAL GUIDE TO FREELANCE WRITING SUCCESS
BY LINDA FORMICHELLI AND DIANA BURRELL, $14.95

ORDER AT WWW.MARIONSTREETPRESS.COM
OR CALL TOLL-FREE 866-443-7987